UNFAIR ADVANTAGE:

SEXUAL ABUSE by
PSYCHOTHERAPISTS,
PRIESTS, AND POLICE

TERRI AUSTIN, PH.D., J.D.

Order this book online at www.trafford.com
or email orders@trafford.com

Most Trafford titles are also available at major online book retailers.

Print information available on the last page.

ISBN: 978-1-4251-0475-7 (sc)

Trafford rev. 01/13/2021

www.trafford.com
North America & international
toll-free: 844-688-6899 (USA & Canada)
fax: 812 355 4082

CONTENTS

PART THREE: INTERVENTION

ACKNOWLEDGEMENTS

The author would like to acknowledge the following people:

- The survivors of abuse for sharing their experiences and having the courage to come forward;

- The victims' attorneys who advocate zealously on behalf of their clients;

- Trafford Publishing;

- SNAP founder Barbara Blaine, Executive Director David Clohessey and Regional Director Mary Grant for their support;

- Police officers who have the courage not to abide by the Code of Silence with regard to professionals who have sexually abused children;

- Friends & colleagues;

The author is grateful to the following publishers, authors, copyright holders and others for granting permission to use excerpts from the following works:

American Psychiatric Association. (1994). *Diagnostic and Statistical Manual of Mental Disorders*, 4th Ed.

National Association of School Psychologists. (2000) *Principles for Professional Ethics Guidelines for the Provision of School Psychological Services*

National Center for Missing and Exploited Children. (1992). *Child Molesters: A Behavioral Analysis for Law*

Enforcement Officers Investigating Cases of Child Sexual Explaoitation, 3rd Ed. Author: Kenneth V. Lanning, Supervisory Special Agent, Department of Justice

The Police Complaint Center www.policeabuse.org 1220 L Street NW Ste. #100-164 Washington, D.C. 20005 (202) 250-3499

The Survivors Network of Those Abused by Priests www.snapnetwork.org

INTRODUCTION

This book is about trusted professionals in mental health, religious, and law enforcement fields who exploit and abuse children and young adults, and the people and institutions who enable these perpetrators by covering up their crimes. While sexual abuse by anyone in a professional capacity is in and of itself a disgrace to those professions and can result in serious damage to victims, sexual offenses committed by priests, psychotherapists, and police officers, results in extremely devastating damage to the victims due to the level of trust implied and inherent in these professions.

For the purposes of this book, "young adults" will be defined as individuals who have attained the legal age of consent up to and including age twenty-five. Research has shown that areas of the human brain which facilitate responsible decision-making and inhibit risk-taking behaviors are not developed in their entirety until approximately the early to mid-twenties. Therefore, a person who has reached the chronological age of twenty-five might be functioning at an immature level and as a result may be vulnerable to suggestions made by others whose intent is to harm.

Sexual predators continue to be the stereotypical strangers who hang around near elementary schools and parks and entice children, via the use of candy or pets—e.g. "Come see my puppy..."— to get into the car with them. They are the child abductors who kidnap children from their home or elsewhere, rape and kill them, as has occurred in many child abduction cases in the United States. Many sexual predators still look every bit the part of the stereotypical "bad guys," and are predominantly male. In recent years, however, female offenders are emerging particularly in the teaching and child care professions. Society has come to realize that the "bad guys" who commit sex offenses are all too frequently trusted individuals v. strangers ---relatives, teachers, school personnel, babysitters, scout leaders, and clergy. Unfortunately, in the absence of criminal convictions specifically for sex crimes against children, there is no way to identify sexual predators or to determine in advance who is predestined to become one.

This book will pertain to the trusted professional who seduces and solicits his victim into becoming involved in a "relationship", versus the perpetrator who forcibly rapes his victim. The emphasis will be on the deliberate planning by the perpetrator prior to, during, and after the commission of the crime. Federal Bureau of Investigation profilers categorize this type of offender as an "organized seduction molester."

This book is intended to be a resource for:

- Victims and survivors of professional exploitation and abuse: to validate and their experiences and facilitate their healing.

- Students of psychology and social work: although this book is not meant to be a textbook, it may be used to supplement course curriculum.

- Police: to emphasize to newly-sworn officers, administrators, and internal affairs investigators the degree of public trust placed in the badge, and the ease with which that trust can be betrayed;

- School Personnel: to enable them to recognize signs which may be indicative that a student is being sexually abused, or that a faculty or staff person may be a sexual predator.

- Parents: to alert them to symptoms which may be indicative that their child(ren) may be the target of a trusted individual.

- The public: to expose sexual predators' modus operandi and tactics for avoiding apprehension for their crimes for as long as decades. It is important that society realize that changes need to be made with regard to statutes of limitations and other legal loopholes which give offenders more rights than victims.

"Unfair advantage" refers to the imbalance of power in a relationship—typically one involving a professional and a person who is in a position of having to trust that individual with matters pertaining to his or her well-being and best interest. "Unfair advantage" will also refer to the (mis)use of the position of power to conceal crimes; the breach of fiduciary duty involved in the process of sexually abusing a client and/or layperson; and the betrayal of the implied trust in the professional position.

This book is a work of non-fiction and the culmination of the author's twenty-five years of research into the behavior of perpetrators of sexual abuse and its impact on the victims. The author has interviewed and advocated on behalf of hundreds of victims, over the years. The author has also interviewed many offenders in prisons and mental health facilities, as well as a few sex offenders who managed never to be arrested or convicted, for the purpose of gaining insight into the criminal mind. Actual cases will be described based on victims and survivors accounts and information from court records. In order to protect the victims' privacy, some of the names and locations have been changed and will be indicated as such by an asterisk. Likewise, some of the events in certain cases have been reconstructed so as to maintain victim confidentiality. These cases are a very small representative sample of hundreds of thousands of incidents of abuse by professionals.

The author expects that this book will not be well-received by sexual predators or their enablers. Individuals who are in denial about the fact that trusted professionals are capable of committing such atrocious crimes might also have difficulty accepting the reality that the events described in this book occur on a daily basis throughout the world.

PROLOGUE

*Carol, age 24, described to her therapist how she had been sexually abused for a number of years, beginning when she was a Middle School student. She indicated that she felt hopeless about her situation and especially her attempt to get the police to investigate. In a recent session with her therapist, the therapist turned the speaker phone on in her office so that Carol could listen to a conversation between the therapist and a police detective who had received the Suspected Child Abuse Report from Child Protective Services and was supposed to be investigating the case. The therapist deliberately informed the detective earlier that day that she would be available by phone during Carol's scheduled therapy appointment; however, she did not inform the detective that Carol would be present and listening to the conversation. The conversation went as follows:

> Detective: "I'm calling to speak with you about a report which you made to Child Protective Services, regarding sexual abuse of Carol occurring when she was in Middle School."

> Therapist: "Yes—-I'm concerned about the possibility of other victims."

> Detective: "When was the last time you met with Carol?"

> Therapist: "She was in today."

> Detective: "What is your impression of her?"

> Therapist: "I'm not sure what you mean…"

> Detective: "We believe she is filing a false report." The de-

tective went on to cite a couple of "previous false reports" allegedly filed by Carol, which Carol knew nothing about.

Therapist: "I believe that she is highly credible. Have you talked to her?

Detective: "No. Do you know her work schedule?"
Therapist: "She works during the day."

Detective: "I'll have to schedule an evening appointment to talk to her. Thank you for your time."

The detective never contacted Carol.

The sexual predator: *Dr. Smith, a clinical psychologist, consultant to the same police department, and friend of the detective assigned to investigate the case.

Carol's attorney, who was in the process of filing a civil lawsuit against Dr. Smith, advised her to bypass the police department and take her case directly to the District Attorney. He had seen this type of situation many times before and knew that the police department was where the ball would be very likely to stop. As predicted, the police never took the time or went out of their way to get a statement from Carol. Ironically, Carol lived only five blocks from the police department.

PART ONE:

THE ABUSERS

CHAPTER ONE:

PSYCHODYNAMICS OF ABUSE

A DEFINITION OF ABUSE

Legal definitions of "child abuse," in general, vary between States with regard to conduct that constitutes child abuse, maltreatment, and exploitation. Mistreatment of human beings by other humans can assume many different forms including physical, sexual, psychological, and emotional and can be classified as criminal, non-criminal, and unethical.

For the purposes of this book, definitions of sexual abuse will include the following and will apply whether or not there is discernable harmful outcome:

- Forcible Rape: Sexual acts with another person against that person's will or knowledge;

- Statutory Rape: Sex with a minor under the legal age of consent, whether or not the child initiated the contact;

- An adult exposing a child to pornography to include viewing or participation in it;

- Any contacts between an adult and a child when the child is used as an object of sexual gratification for the adult. This constitutes abuse whether or not explicit force is used and whether or not genital or physical contact occurs;

- Psychological sexual abuse, [aka, "psycho-sexual abuse"], which is the type of abuse that is based primarily on psychological and emotional manipulation of the victim by the perpetrator with regard to a "love" relationship; may involve non-sexual although suggestive physical contact; and may eventually culminate in sexual contact of some sort.

- Solicitation and seduction via the internet, whether or not any actual physical contact occurs;

Psychological sexual abuse is typically the first phase of what is referred to as the "grooming process" of the victim by the perpetrator. The perpetrator is usually a trusted adult who has known the victim for a period of time and who encourages the victim to develop a "crush" on him or her, or does not discourage an existing "crush." Dependency by the victim is reinforced via compliments, flirting, promises, gifts, letters, etc., on the part of the perpetrator. Control is exerted over the victim in a psychological and emotional sense in that the victim is made to believe that (s)he is "special" and that a "special relationship" exists between the perpetrator and victim which, in reality, does not exist.

IT'S ALL ABOUT POWER

The following elements are required in order for exploitation and abuse by professionals and/or institutions to occur:

1. A relationship exists which is based on an imbalance of power; for example student-teacher, psychotherapist-client, doctor-patient, employer-employee, priest-layperson; in most cases, a fiduciary duty of some sort exists on the part of the professional;

2. An element of trust is present on the part of the person with the lesser degree of power, which is eventually betrayed;

3. The professional takes unfair advantage of the trusting person sexually, financially, or emotionally;

4.   The institution whose responsibility it is to support and
     protect the victim instead assists the perpetrator in de-
     nying and covering up the behavior and blaming the
     victim, or chooses to ignore the victim and does not
     provide any intervention;

Abuse by professionals involves a misuse of power. What is
"power"? It is the authority that is inherent in certain positions or
organizations. When someone or some institution has the authority to influence the lives, behavior, perception, and reality of others who do not have the same level of authority, that is "power." In
most professions a standard of care and duty exist which constitute
the level of conduct required of professionals to avoid harming
others either physically, emotionally, or financially and incurring
liability. Malpractice laws exist in all States to prohibit the professional from benefiting at the client's expense through intentional
or negligent breach of duty to the client. In determining violations of standards of care, courts generally look at factors such as
the professional's degree of training, education, and special skills.
Individuals with advanced training and education, and who have
certification as to special skills, are typically held to a higher standard of care than the average person.

Everyone in positions of power has a duty not to harm others
who depend on them for assistance. This is particularly true of
physicians, attorneys, teachers, and priests. Breaches of duty and
abuse of power can occur criminally and non-criminally. Non-
criminal breaches of duty and trust are usually considered to be
professional ethics violations, the sanctions for which do not include imprisonment.

Non-criminal and therefore non-arrestable types of sexual
abuse usually involve a professional and another adult----usually
a young, or otherwise vulnerable, adult. It can include implied
and covert sexual conduct, where actual sexual contact may not be

present but the breach of trust and misuse of power exist nonetheless. This type of sexual abuse can be equally damaging as that consisting of physical contact. It includes an element of infliction of emotional distress by the professional toward the victim, in that there is a reckless disregard on the part of the professional as to whether the victim will suffer emotional upset as the result of his or her conduct. In these cases, civil liability can still exist even if the perpetrator had no intention of causing the emotional distress simply based on the unequal power in the relationship. Other examples of unethical and non-criminal conduct include verbal and/or behavioral manipulations, coercive verbal persuasion just short of actual threats; and sexual conduct which may appear to be between consenting adults but, in actuality, due to the nature of the relationship one of the adults is technically unable to give consent—at least not informed consent. This kind of sexual conduct is often the result of coercion, lies, and various kinds of manipulation by the professional so as to persuade the victim to participate. Similar tactics are used to financially exploit victims-—tactics just short of actual fraud—e.g., playing on the victim's sense of obligation and fears of abandonment. In these situations, it appears that the victim is voluntarily giving his or her money to the perpetrator but in actuality (s)he is not.

CHARACTERISTICS OF SEXUAL PREDATORS

During a discussion in one of my Forensic Psychology courses, a student asked, "What kind of an adult actually enjoys having sex with kids?" I invited class participation with regard to speculation of the answer to that question. Responses included: "Someone with a perverted mind; a person who can't make it with another adult; a wimp; an asshole; somebody who should be locked up; an adult who doesn't care about kids, or anybody else besides himself; a control-freak; somebody who is fixated at a child's level and hasn't really grown up; guys who hate women; people with lousy interpersonal boundaries; people with severe mental problems; someone who knows what he is doing, but thinks he won't get caught; a person who knows how to lie his way out of getting caught; people who commit crimes, like those serial killers you hear about; a sick son-of-a-bitch; somebody who should be locked up and the key thrown away."

The correct answer? All of the above.

There is no single characteristic identifying individuals who are child sexual predators. Rather, a combination of factors and characteristics contributes to the overall problem. Unfortunately, identification of the predators usually happen only after they have committed the crime.

* * * * * * * *

PERSONALITY DISORDERS

Certain of the Personality Disorders described in the *Diagnostic and Statistical Manual of Mental Disorders IV* (American Psychiatric Association, 1994) have consistently been associated with individuals who commit sex crimes. Personality disorders, as compared with personality traits, encompass enduring patterns of inflexible behaviors which remain pervasive in social and personal situations. *DSM-IV* defines personality disorders in general as: an enduring pattern of inner experience and behavior that deviates markedly from the expectations of the individual's culture, manifested in at least two of the following areas:

Cognition: ways of perceiving and interpreting other people, self, and events;

Affectivity: the range, intensity, lability, and appropriateness of emotional response;

Interpersonal functioning: manners of interacting with others;

Impulse control: the ability to delay immediate gratification.

Personality Disorders comprise a separate axis of a five-axis diagnosis as established by *DSM-IV* (APA, 1994). While they certainly have an effect on a person's ability to function effectively in life, personality disorders are to be distinguished from other mental and emotional illnesses in that the latter tend to be responsive to medications and therapy. Individuals with personality disorders rarely seek therapy unless required to do so by third parties—e.g., a court ordering therapy as a condition of probation—because they are insensitive to, and often could care less about, the impact that their behavior has on others. They will usually deny that they have a problem, while maintaining an "Everybody else has a problem but me," attitude. Traditional types of psychotherapy tend to be ineffective for those who attend therapy sessions due to the fact that these people have difficulty forming a therapeutic bond with a therapist.

A couple of the Personality Disorders are especially more prone to violence and abuse than others. Specifically, these are the Antisocial, and Narcissistic, Personality Disorders.

Antisocial Personality Disorder

DSM-IV (APA, 1994) describes this disorder as follows:

A pervasive pattern of disregard for and violation of the rights of others occurring since age 15 years, as indicated by at least three of the following when committed by a person at least 18 years of age:

- Failure to conform to social norms with respect to lawful behaviors as indicated by repeatedly performing acts that are grounds for arrest;

- Deceitfulness, as indicated by repeated lying, use of aliases, or conning others for personal profit or pleasure;

- Impulsivity and failure to plan ahead;

- Irritability and aggressiveness, as indicated by repeated physical fights or assaults;

- Reckless disregard for the of self or others;

- Consistent irresponsibility, as indicated by repeated failure to sustain consistent work behavior or honor financial responsibilities;

- Lack of remorse, as indicated by being indifferent to or rationalizing having hurt, mistreated, or stolen from another.

[Copyright 2000 by the American Psychiatric Association, Wasington, D.C. Use of this material is by permission of the publisher. www.apa.org.]

Most of the inmates in prisons and on Death Row are doing time because of repeated and habitual conduct associated with this disorder. For the majority of inmates with this disorder, prison is their second if not primary home. They think that the law doesn't or shouldn't apply to them; laws are an inconvenience—a big monkey wrench in their lifestyle. While many of us might not feel too badly about committing minor violations of the law which don't hurt anyone else—e.g., not stopping for a red light at 3:00 a.m. at a remote intersection at which there is no traffic whatsoever—this person thinks nothing of driving in excess of the speed limit while heavily under the influence of drugs and/or alcohol at any time of the day or night. People with Antisocial Personality Disorder feel very little or no remorse or guilt over repeatedly committing crimes which would result in harm to others, since individuals with Antisocial Personality Disorder are significantly lacking a sense of conscience.

Since the Antisocial individual operates on the basis of a significant lack of conscience and, therefore, cannot be trusted, he will have no problem looking you straight in the eye and lying—and then looking you straight in the eye and deny having lied if confronted about lying. He will try to convince you that there is something wrong with you for doubting his story, and that you have hurt his feelings for not believing him. You can expect wall-to-wall bullshit from this person, as he will say whatever it takes to get whatever he wants. If he admits to having lied, he will state that it is someone else's or your fault that he had to lie. He is highly adept at "scamming" people out of money and property. He will tell his victims what he thinks they want to hear. For example, if he knows his intended victim is interested in exotic plants, he will pretend to be an "expert" at or "very interested in" exotic plants even though he might actually be disinterested in horticulture altogether.

The individual with this disorder uses people for his own ends without consideration as to resulting harm. He is aware of but prefers to disregard the possible consequences of his behavior. His main priority pertains to immediate satisfaction. He has very poor impulse control and finds it difficult if not impossible to delay gratification. Domestic violence, child abuse, animal abuse, theft, and property damage are not uncommon behaviors of this person. He is quick-tempered and becomes easily angered at the most seemingly insignificant matters, and is easily provoked into fighting. The Antisocial Personality is capable of cold-blooded premeditated torture or murder and, in the process, becoming angry at the victim's attempts to resist or escape. In his sick mind, he perceives the victim as inconveniencing him in the commission of his crime. Subsequently, he can discuss the incident as casually as though he were discussing the weather conditions. An example of this is Gary Ridgway, the "Green River Killer" who, in a Dateline NBC interview, displayed no emotion whatsoever as he casually described the process by which he murdered his victims. Ridgway may just as well have been reciting items from a grocery list. If the Antisocial individual commits murder and denies it, he will attempt to make it appear as though someone else committed it, such as California killer Scott Peterson's attempt to blame the murder of his wife and unborn son on several homeless people in his neighborhood on the night of the murder. Some will actually go to the trouble of attempting to frame someone else to be arrested based on circumstantial evidence of the crime.

There are many hypotheses as to causality of Antisocial Personality Disorder, however scientific empirical research into the validity of these hypotheses has been very insufficient. Most of the hypotheses propose a correlation between Antisocial Personality Disorder and dysfunctional families of origin. It is important to remember that not every child from dysfunctional families will develop Conduct Disorder (which is, in effect, the characteristics of Antisocial Personality Disorder with an onset prior to age 18) or Antisocial Personality Disorder. The problem with the assumption that the disorder is "caused' by dysfunctional family environments is that an extremely critical variable is not acknowledged: most individuals with this disorder make conscious, deliberate choices to engage in the conduct which meets the *DSM-IV* criteria. Stanton Samenow (2004) discusses this issue in depth in his book *Inside the Criminal Mind, 2nd Edition*. It is possible for three out of four children in a dysfunctional family not to engage in criminal conduct simply because they have consciously chosen to behave appropriately.

Additional attempts to explain the causes of Antisocial Personality Disorder have included the following:

- Physical, emotional, and sexual abuse by parents;

- Physical, emotional, and educational neglect by parents;

- Inadequate or complete absence of supervision—e.g., latchkey kids, single-parent households;

- Families with low socio-economic status;

- Excessively-strict parents; in many of these situations delinquent behavior is a form of rebellion;

- Criminal lifestyle within the family of origin —e.g., substance abuse, gang affiliation, etc.;

- Peer pressure;

- Excessively-indulgent parents;

- Violence as an accepted method for solving problems in the home;

- Exposure to excessive violence on TV and in video games.

While all of these factors may be contributing factors in the onset of juvenile and adult crime, it is important to realize that no single factor—but rather a combination of them—can contribute to transient forms of juvenile delinquency, Conduct Disorder, and Antisocial Personality Disorder.

Narcissistic Personality Disorder

DSM-IV (APA, 1994) describes this disorder as follows:

A pervasive pattern of grandiosity (in fantasy or behavior), need for admiration, and lack of empathy, beginning by early adulthood and present in a variety of contexts, as indicated by at least five of the following:

- Has a grandiose sense of self-importance (e.g., exaggerates achievements and talents, and expects to be recognized as superior without commensurate achievements);

- Is preoccupied with fantasies of unlimited success, power, brilliance, beauty, or ideal love;

- Believes that (s)he is "special" and unique and can only be understood by, or should associate with, other special or high-status individuals or institutions;

- Requires excessive admiration;

- Has a sense of entitlement, i.e., unreasonable expectations of especially favorable treatment or automatic compliance with his or her expectations;

- Is interpersonally exploitative, i.e., takes advantage of others to achieve his or her own ends;

- Lacks empathy: is unwilling to recognize or identify with the feelings or needs of others;

- Is often envious of others or believes that others are envious of him or her;

- Shows arrogant, haughty behaviors or attitudes.

It has been hypothesized that a significant loss(es) in childhood, which is/are disruptive to a child's self-esteem, is the most crucial variable associated with the development of Narcissistic Personality Disorder.

There is considerable overlap between the criteria for Antisocial and Narcissistic Personality Disorders. Like the Antisocial, the Narcissist often doesn't care who gets hurt as the result of his behavior, and will act in disregard of the possible effects of his behavior on himself or others. For example, individuals with this disorder who are in gangs will take risks in dangerous situations, thinking that they won't get hurt, and not caring about anybody else who might, as typically happens in drive-by shootings resulting in the deaths of innocent bystanders. Driving under the influence of drugs or alcohol with children in the car is another example of this. Similarly, the Narcissist will attempt to blame others for the consequences or results of his own behavior, and will even claim to be the victim of his own crimes.

The Narcissist believes that he is a highly-important person and superior to everybody else. He thinks that anything he does is better than what others do. For example, a student having written an average-quality thesis expects that it deserves at least an "A+" grade. An attractive woman with this disorder might think that she should be Miss Universe. The founder of a particular business may attempt to put other similar types of agencies out of business. (S)he is constantly in competition with others—and often unbeknownst to others—to be the "best" or the "one and only."

The Narcissist is a "power-tripper" and control-freak. It is common for these individuals to be employed in top-management positions, or occupations such as priests, ministers, surgeons, and psychotherapists. When working as part of a committee, the Narcissist will attempt to put others down so as to make himself appear more important or favorable than the other committee members. His over-sensitivity to criticism or anything which he perceives as negative feedback or seemingly disparaging remarks borders on paranoia. His own set of unrealistic "standards" which regular, "inferior" people do not live up to because the standards are usually unrealistic and impossible to live up to, justify diminishing these people and their efforts. He believes that people are at his disposal and beck and call. Therefore, he expects them to respond accordingly, immediately, and without question. He comes across as arrogant and unapproachable. He detaches from his own emotions, fearing them and believing that emotions are a sign of "weakness."

The Narcissist needs to be the center of attention. Constantly. He believes he is entitled to "steal someone else's thunder" so as to be the star of the show. This reminds me of a client of mine who described how, at his sixth grade school Christmas Pageant in which he was to play a piano solo, his narcissistic father competed with him by attending the pageant dressed to the nines in his West Point military officer uniform, while all of the other parents wore semi-formal or casual attire. There was no reason for the man to have been in uniform; it wasn't as though he had just stepped off a plane and did not have sufficient time to change clothes prior to the start of the pageant. This had a minimizing effect on the child's piano solo in that people were commenting that the pianist was "the son of the man in the uniform" and "Wow—look at *Johnny's dad!—doesn't he look sharp?" The boy's father managed to compete with his son to the extent of making himself the focus of the audience at his son's pageant.

Case Example: Serial Killer Ted Bundy

Referred to as the "poster boy" of serial killers, Ted Bundy is the classic example of co-morbidity between Antisocial and Narcissistic Personality Disorders. Like the Antisocial, the Narcissist is a smooth-talker; a silver-tongued devil adept at persuasion, manipulation, and lying. This describes Ted Bundy to a tee.

Theodore Robert Bundy's mom gave birth to him at the age of approximately twenty-one years. She assumed the role of "older sister" versus "mother" in raising him.

As a teenager, Bundy reportedly was an excellent student at his high school. He was also a member of the Boy Scouts, and very active in his church. Peers and teachers eventually became aware that he had a bad temper. His criminal behaviors began prior to high school with petty crimes such as shoplifting. Eventually, his crimes progressed to carjacking, burglary, and "peeping Tom" activities.

Bundy eventually went on to attend law school and campaigned for the Washington Republican Party. He also volunteered at a suicide prevention center.

Bundy was the type of killer that the FBI calls an "organized serial killer." He deliberately and carefully planned his crimes in terms of the method by which he would manipulate and con his victims, kill them, and dispose of the bodies and other evidence. His preferred victims were young Caucasian females with long dark hair parted down the middle. Police arrested Bundy when his vehicle was recognized as one which fit the description of the suspect wanted for kidnapping and murder.

At both of his trials, Bundy insisted on representing himself as his own attorney. He was convicted and the judge sentenced him to death. While on Death Row, Bundy continued to manipulate the system by offering his assistance to law enforcement investigators in locating bodies of his victims. He also offered to assist in the apprehension of the Green River Killer. As his execution date became closer, Bundy attempted to postpone his execution by confessing to additional murders and promising to disclose the locations of the disposal sites of these bodies. A stay of execution was denied and Bundy was executed in Florida State Prison's electric chair as scheduled.

After years of adamant denial, just prior to his execution in

1989, this handsome, intelligent, silver-tongued devil finally admitted to killing at least 36 women in different States between 1974 and 1978. His final victim in 1978 was a 12-year old girl.

EXPLANATIONS FOR SEXUAL ABUSE

Psycho-Analytic

Sigmund Freud (1856-1939) believed that sexual urges were the basis of people's instinctual drives. According to Freud's theory it can be presumed that an overly dominant super-ego is to an extent responsible for behavior which constitutes child abuse.

Low Self-Esteem

Other research on child sexual abuse has stated that sexual predators' conduct is based on an extremely low self-esteem. By exerting dominance over child victims, they attempt to compensate for real or imagined lack of power and control.

Sexual Attraction to Children:

This attraction may result from an individual's early sexual experiences as a pre-pubescent child or as an adolescent. As (s) he becomes older, the individual continues to remain sexually attracted to children, rather than developing an attraction to adults.

Misinterpretation of Children's Affection:

Affectionate behavior expressed by children—e.g., hugging, hand-holding, kissing etc—is often misinterpreted by certain adults as flirting, or solicitation, and they respond to these innocent behaviors in a sexual manner. Since their psychosexual development has been arrested at a child's level, they select victims who are at an emotional level which they believe they can relate to—that is, children.

Poor Impulse Control:

Certain adults who are sexually attracted to children have very poor impulse control. This is not to say that they cannot control their impulses. Rather, they make the conscious choice not to do so despite awareness of the criminal sanctions which would be imposed if and when the behavior comes to the attention of authorities.

PEDOPHILES, EPHEBOPHILES, AND CHILD MOLESTERS

The term "pedophile" has been commonly used for years as a catch-all term for individuals who molest children. In actuality, the term "pedophile (pedophilia)" comes from the *DSM-IV* (APA, 1994), and refers to an individual who has recurrent, intense, sexually arousing fantasies, urges, or self-stimulating behaviors involving pre-pubescent children, occurring over a period of at least 6 months (APA, 1994). This in and of itself is a paraphilia—a type of psychological disorder—and not a sexual abuse crime. Some pedophiles engage in only fantasy, or will act-out fantasies in legal ways—e.g., talking to children in public places, or watching children play—while others will act on those fantasies and sexually abuse children. Technically, if the fantasy is not acted-out illegally, the pedophile is not a child molester. Individuals with this particular type of paraphilia who have no desire to change their behavior and who are not "markedly distressed" by their feelings and/or conduct will not seek therapy on a voluntary basis.

Ephebophelia is an attraction by an adult to post-pubescent adolescents. As with pedophilia, ephebophilia refers to the feelings, fantasies, and urges as opposed to actual physical contact.

Each state varies with regard to the legal age of consent. Therefore, whenever a situation exists in which the partner of an adult is below the legal age of consent, sexual activity between these individuals meets the criteria for statutory rape. This law applies even if the minor initiated, or appears to be a willing participant in, the activity.

The United States Department of Justice and the National Center for Missing and Exploited Children identify two basic sub-categories of child molesters:

Situational

The situational molester does not have a true sexual preference for children but will look to children for sexual gratification for a variety of situational reasons. Often, these molesters will substitute children for their preferred adult sexual partners. Sometimes, they will choose to sexually abuse children just because the opportunity exists and they think that they can get away with it (DOJ, NCMEC, 1992)

Preferential

These are the true child molesters who actually prefer children over adult sex partners. These individuals tend to be more intelligent than situational molesters and may even come from higher socio-economic groups. Their sexually abusive behavior is usually scripted, compulsive, and fantasy-driven, often involving the use of web-cams, digital camera, camcorders, and computers. They are also gender-specific and age-specific with regard to their choice of victims (DOJ, NCMEC, 1992).

A preferential child molester can be identified by the following behaviors (DOJ, NCMEC, 1992):

- A pattern, beginning in early adolescence, of having an unusual interest in younger children;

- While maturing, their life centers around being with children;

- Willingness to commit large amounts of money, energy, and time interacting with children;

- Has developed techniques for complete access to many victims (e.g., is a member of the North American Man-Boy Love Association, an organization which promotes sexual relationships between adults and children);

- Rationalizes that sexual interests in children are not harmful, are consensual, and are even beneficial for the child;

- Is able to lie and manipulate very skillfully;

- Often records child sexual fantasies in computer files or journals;

- Maintains a collection of child pornography;

- Utilizes pornography to lower the victim's inhibitions;

- Collects "souvenirs" from the molestation incidents;

- Targets specific victims by age and gender characteristics;

- Makes efforts to turn fantasies into reality.

> [Copyright 2000 by the National Center for Missing and Exploited Children. *Child Molesters: A Behavioral Analysis for Law Enforcement Officers Investigating Cases of Child Sexual Exploitation, 3rd Ed.* Author: Kenneth V. Lanning, Supervisory Special Agent, Department of Justice. Use of this material is by per-

mission of the publisher. wwwmissingkids.com]

It is interesting to note that, in the absence of symptoms and conditions meeting the legal criteria for "insanity", the mindset of child molesters is identical to that of the serial killer: conscious choices are made to sexually abuse a child. An element of pre-med itation and planning exists. The behavior is repeated with a time-lapse of varying lengths between incidents. "Souvenirs" might be taken by the perpetrator from each incident. Attempts are made to conceal the crime. As with serial killers, child molesters can be of the "organized" and "unorganized" types. The latter tends to spend very little time planning the offense and concealing the evidence. Many single-incident sexual assaults and rape-murders are committed by the unorganized predator. In contrast, the organized predator devotes a considerable amount of time selecting and grooming his victims and attempting to conceal the crimes.

While the act of homicide in and of itself may not necessarily always constitute a crime in that there are justifiable and excusable homicides such as those occurring in situations of self-defense or by accidental means, there is NO justification or excuse which renders the act of child sexual abuse legal

THE NORTH AMERICAN
MAN-BOY LOVE ASSOCIATION

There is an organization in the United States which promotes sexual relationships between men and boys, and which the FBI has attempted for years to stop: the organization calls itself NAMBLA—the North American Man-Boy Love Association. They attempt to justify their mission by referring to the behavior it promotes as "inter-generational sex", versus "child abuse," or "statutory rape."

NAMBLA is involved in the following:

- Distribution of child pornography;

- Publication of *The Survival Manual: The Man's Guide to Staying Alive in Man-Boy Sexual Relationships* , which is basically an "instruction manual" for stalking and grooming victims, and grooming the victim's parents and the community. It also advises sexual predators as to their options in the event that they are discovered and arrested.

NAMBLA was founded in 1978—one of the founders being Father Paul Shanley, a Catholic priest who is alleged to have molested at least twenty-six children as young as six-years-old for several decades. Many of NAMBLA's members are lawyers, teachers, judges, clergy, and other professionals. The organization claims not to condone coercive sexual abuse. However, in 1997, two NAMBLA members were convicted for the kidnapping, rape, torture, mutilation, and murder of a ten-year-old boy.

Case Example: NAMBLA Members Convicted of Murder

A ten-year-old victim was stalked by two NAMBLA members, Charlie Jaynes and Salvatore Sicari, kidnapped via promises of a new bike, raped, and suffocated with a gasoline-soaked rag. After the victim was dead, Jaynes reportedly sodomized his body. Jaynes is incarcerated at Massachusetts Correctional Institution and has received cash donations from NAMBLA members since his incarceration.

The victim's parents filed a lawsuit for civil damages against NAMBLA in 2000. NAMBLA was defended by the American Civil Liberties Union, which prevailed in a dismissal of the lawsuit on the grounds that NAMBLA is not a corporation, but an association. The victim's parents continued to pursue the case in court as a wrongful death action against NAMBLA, and the ACLU continued to defend NAMBLA, alleging First Amendment rights violation by the lawsuit as a defense. The ACLU denies any endorsement of NAMBLA's promotion of child abuse or their opposition of sexual-consent laws.

* * * * * * * * * *

THE INSANITY DEFENSE

"Insanity" in and of itself is a legal term and not a medical or psychological term. The term "insanity" is not one for which the *DSM-IV* provides diagnostic criteria. In fact, the *DSM-IV* contains a disclaimer in the front section of the book which states in part (APA, 1994):

> "The specified diagnostic criteria for each mental disorder are offered as guidelines for making diagnoses...they do not encompass all of the conditions for which people may be treated or that may be appropriate topics for research efforts. The clinical and scientific considerations involved in categorization of these conditions as mental disorders may not be wholly relevant to legal judgments, for example, that take in to account such issues as individual responsibility, disability determination, and competency."
>
> [Copyright 2000 by the American Psychiatric Association, Washington, D.C. . Use of this material is by permission of the publisher. www.apa.org.]

Insanity refers to certain criteria which courts have determined may render a defendant who meets these criteria eligible for confinement to a State Hospital for the Criminally Insane versus a traditional prison. Insanity is not the same as a mental disorder, although a mental disorder can be a component of insanity. It is possible for a person to be mentally ill without being insane.

In order to be considered legally insane, a defendant must meet the following criteria:

- Have a defect of reason arising from a disease of the mind resulting in not knowing the nature or quality of the act at the time of commission of the act or, if he did know it, the defendant did not know that the conduct was wrong;

- Defendant, as the result of a mental illness affecting volitional capacity, acted from an irresistible and un-controllable impulse;

Case Example: Serial Killer Jeffery Dahmer

Society will not easily forget the case of Jeffery Dahmer, the serial killer who, between 1978 and 1991, cannibalized his male victims and had sex with their corpses until discovered by police in 1991. Dahmer preferred gay Asian and African American men and would solicit his victims in gay bars, inviting them back to his apartment where he would serve them alcoholic beverages containing sedating drugs. Dahmer would proceed to sexually assault his victims and, at the point when they began to lose consciousness from the sedating drugs, kill them. He would then dismember the victims' corpse, keep certain of the body parts as souvenirs, and dispose of the remains by dissolving them in acid. Dahmer would spray-paint skulls of some of his victims so as to make the skulls appear artificial. These skulls were kept in plain view in his bedroom and throughout his apartment.

Dahmer's bizarre behavior began during adolescence. He had an interest in dead animals, and would often torture and kill animals so as to collect their skulls and body parts. He committed his first murder when he was eighteen years old, and developed an interest in necrophile behavior. Necrophilia—sexual activity with a corpse—is not uncommon in individuals who have an excessive need to control people and who are unable to maintain appropriate relationships with living persons.

In 1991, one of Dahmer's victims escaped from Dahmer's apartment and reported Dahmer's activities to the police. When police arrived at Dahmer's apartment they found the remains of eleven victims, bodies decaying in barrels of acid, and severed heads and other human body parts in the refrigerator and freezer

At his trial, Dahmer entered a plea of "guilty but insane." The jury spent considerable time attempting to determine whether or not Dahmer met the legal criteria for "insanity." Based on the fact that, at the time he committed each offense, he understood the nature of his behavior, could distinguish between right and wrong, was capable of controlling his actions, and devoted a significant amount of time in the planning of each murder and the conceal- ment of evidence, the court determined that he was not insane. Dahmer was sentenced to fifteen consecutive life sentences— which comes out to at least 936 years in prison. Had the State of Wisconsin been pro-capital punishment at the time, Dahmer would definitely have received the death penalty.

In 1994 Dahmer and another inmate were murdered in prison by a gang of inmates. The leader of this gang was an psychotic inmate who had delusions that he was Jesus Christ, and claimed to be acting out God his "father's" instructions to kill Dahmer, so as to help rid the world of homosexuals.

TERRI AUSTIN, PH.D., J.D.

NOTES:

Notes:

CHAPTER TWO:

SEXUAL PREDATORS' MODUS OPERANDI: A CONTINUING PROCESS

GROOMING THE VICTIM

There are many elements to the modus operandi of a sexual predator who is also a trusted professional, and it is an ongoing process which does not stop when the initial sexual abuse occurs, but continues indefinitely thereafter.

The typical sexual abuse process by a professional might proceed as follows:

Attraction to A Child, Teenager, or Young Adult.

Usually, when sexual abuse by a professional occurs, the victim and predator are not strangers. They have interacted in some manner over a period of time as the result of the perpetrator's professional status. Quite often, the professional has been a trusted friend of the family.

Predator Grooms the Victim.

This happens over a period of days, months, or even years. It typically begins as a non-sexual friendship between the professional and the victim. The professional will take the victim on outings, buy expensive gifts for him or her, and even provide alcohol or drugs. Dependency on the professional by the victim is encouraged and reinforced as a means of breaking down the victim's emotional and psychological defenses. Trust is further established when the professional plays the role of an emphatic listener with regard to the victim's complaints about a negative home environment, conflicts with parents, or other troubling matter. The victim is told that (s)he can feel free to talk to the professional about anything at any time without having to fear disclosure. At some point, the professional states or implies to the victim that they have a "special relationship." In cases where the victim is a minor, the professional might even tell the victim that (s)he is "waiting" for him or her to become of legal age so that "more can come of the relationship". This serves to create a false sense of intimacy on the part of the victim. There may also be frequent non-sexual physical contact. To adolescents who may have experienced parental abandonment or loss—whether on a physical or emotional level—this "special relationship" with the professional serves to fill a significant void. At this point, the victim can easily be persuaded to do anything which the professional requests of him/her. In one case involving a fifteen-year-old girl and her married "lover" in his thirties, the victim was persuaded to work as a stripper and prostitute for his sex parties. He eventually persuaded her to kill her parents and thirteen-year-old brother after her parents discovered that she had been in a "relationship" with this man for quite some time.

Internet Grooming

Internet grooming occurs in a similar manner as in-person types of grooming, the main difference being that the sexual predator has access to potential victims via chat rooms designed specifically for child pornography such as "*Cyber Lolita*," "*Child Rape*," and "*I Am Fourteen*." Information is exchanged between predator and victim via the chat room. Predators will provide false information in the chat rooms and even post photographs which they allege to be of themselves but which, in actuality, may be of someone else. Eventually, a meeting place and time is arranged between predator and victim for the purpose of sexual activity.

Many sexual predators have been arrested as the result of law enforcement programs which are designed to catch these predators in the act of soliciting sex with minors. One such program has been featured on *Dateline NBC* [*www.msnbc.com*].

Case Example: Chat Room Sexual Abuse and Murder

In 2003, homicide suspect Saul Dos Reis pled guilty to federal charges of crossing State lines for the purposes of having sex with a minor. The victim was a thirteen-year-old girl whom he solicited in an online chat room. Dos Reis strangled his victim while they were having sex in his car, and then dumped her body in a ravine. Ironically, while incarcerated, Dos Reis has posted a personal ad on www.inmate.com which includes his photograph, in attempts to solicit female pen-pals.

Case Example: Chat Room Sex Solicitation

An Ohio police chief was arrested in April, 2003, for soliciting sex with a police detective posing as a minor in an online chat room. This occurred within two weeks after he had been sworn-in as Chief of Police. Apparently, the chats were ongoing for approximately a month, unbeknownst to the victim's parents. An officer for the Regional Electronic and Computer Investigations unit of the sheriff's department accidentally discovered the illegal communications while using the Chief's computer.

Case Example: Child Welfare Professionals Identified in Internet Porn

In October, 2002, hundreds of professionals employed in child welfare occupations worldwide were identified as subscribers to internet pornography sites after investigators investigated over 7200 subscribers to internet porn sites in the United States. These professionals included police, teachers, firefighters, and others associated with the criminal justice system—individuals whose job entails the protection of children. The project, known as Operation Avalanche, has identified more than 75,000 online porn subscribers throughout the world, and was originally initiated in Texas by the United States Postal Inspection Service.

Primary abuse

This refers to the actual sexually abusive conduct between the professional and the victim. It includes viewing pornography together, oral sex, sexual touching whether clothed or unclothed, intercourse, sodomy, mutual masturbation, prolonged hugging and kissing.

Secondary abuse

These are behaviors which occur contemporaneous and subsequent to the primary abuse. Included are emotional abuse and the setting-up of the victim by the perpetrator for non-support by individuals and agencies whose job it is to be supportive. This is accomplished by the predator playing on society's denial; by making the victim appear to be non-credible; by making himself out to appear to be a "model citizen"; and by making the victim appear to be the "initiator" by alleging that routine, non-criminal actions by the victim are actually "stalking" behaviors. It is also accomplished by the professional utilizing role-reversal to persuade the victim that maintaining silence and secrecy is crucial to the existence of their "relationship," and instilling a sense of responsibility in the victim for the professional's well-being. Persuasion techniques include threats of harm to the victim, the victim's family, friends, and pets; promises (most of which turn out to be empty); bribes of money, drugs, and other favors; and various psychologically manipulative tactics such as playing on the victim's low self-esteem or fears of abandonment.

GROOMING THE COMMUNITY

Sexual predators who are also trusted professionals will go to great lengths to conceal their crimes and deflect possible suspicion from themselves before, during, and after they have sexually abused their victims. They accomplish this by any or all of the following strategies:

Defamation of victim

By making it appear that the victim is a liar or has severe psychological problems—and doing this without the victim's knowledge—a predator can shift the focus from himself as a potential or possible suspect to the victim as a non-credible source of information. Predators will do this in anticipation of the possibility that the victim decides to report the sexual abuse

Case Example: School Counselor

*Mark was a counselor in a public high school who sexually abused a male student for several years. Prior to initiating sexual contact with the victim, Mark told the school faculty that the academic problems which the victim was experiencing in school were due to Attention Deficit Disorder. He further diagnosed the personality conflicts between the victim and faculty were due to a severe case of Conduct Disorder and Oppositional Defiant Disorder. Unbeknownst to the victim, Mark was also telling other counselors, teachers, the principal, and the dean of students that the victim "had a tendency to make up wild stories" and should not be believed. When the victim finally spoke out about the abuse, initially he was not believed because of his reputation for being a "problem child" as compared with Mark's reputation of being an exemplary employee of the school district.

Appearance of "Model Citizen"

Many sexual predators who are professionals are prominent members of their community. They can be found serving on various committees, and are members of non-profit social and religious organizations. Some have even been given awards for outstanding community service or heroic deeds such as intervening in an emergency situation. The more that the perpetrator can use and embellish this to his advantage, the more difficult it is for the victims of sexual abuse by these professionals to prove their case in the absence of witnesses or corroborating evidence. Priests who molest children have relied on the implied trust of the community with regard to their religious vocation. They have hidden behind their status as representatives of God, over the past few decades, in attempts to discredit their victims' accusations.

Conspiracy with Enablers

It is not uncommon for professionals who sexually abuse children to have friends and or associates who are also professionals enable their crimes. This happens when the enabler is aware of the predator's conduct but does not report it to appropriate authorities, or deliberately attempts to obstruct the investigation of reported incidents. This places the enabler in a position of being a co-conspirator, or an accessory prior to or after the fact, and would subject him or her to criminal sanctions if arrested and convicted.

Notes:

Terri Austin, Ph.D., J.D.

NOTES:

CHAPTER THREE:

ABUSE BY PSYCHOTHERAPISTS

Laws and ethical standards, set forth by professional organizations such as the American Psychological Association and the American Psychiatric Association, exist with regard to providers of psychological services—including psychiatrists, psychologists, social workers, family therapists—so as to protect the public. Issues addressed by these laws and standards include but are not limited to consumer welfare, competency, professional relationships, and advertising and public statements. Regulations also exist pertaining to psychotherapists having sexual relationships with clients, former clients, and relatives of clients. In most States, it is unethical and/or illegal for psychotherapists to provide services to individuals with whom there has been a previous sexual relationship. The violations and breaches of these laws and regulations can constitute professional malpractice and render the professional liable for civil damages and/or criminal sanctions.

Psychotherapists are required to abide by the same Hippocratic Oath as physicians: "Above all, do no harm." Unfortunately, in many cases, more harm than good is done. Clients trust their therapists in terms of their psychological and emotional well-being. They reveal their most personal secrets, feelings, fears, and thoughts to their therapists, trusting the therapist to maintain confidentiality and expecting these mental health professionals to help them resolve issues, overcome emotional obstacles, and facilitate healing—not to inflict further damage.

Some therapists with fragile egos and inadequate or nonexistent interpersonal boundaries will manage to reverse the roles in the relationship, resulting in the client being a caretaker for the therapist—sexually, financially, and emotionally. Mental health professionals who exploit and abuse their clients rely on a type of emotional seduction whereby they simultaneously attempt to give the appearance of filling a void in the client's life while using the client's trust and emotional vulnerabilities to their own advantage. In order for these professionals to maintain an ongoing sexually abusive relationship with a client, **it is imperative that the client *not* make progress toward resolution of psychological and emotional issues** because, if this were to happen, the client would then be in a better position to realize that (s)he has been the victim of abuse and initiate legal action against the professional. By keeping the client in a dependent role and discouraging and even sabotaging increments of progress toward healing, the professional manages to stay in control. This is typically accomplished by means of the following:

Attacking the client's self-esteem:

Verbally abusive comments—e.g., "You are low-class," "I don't think you're able to hold down a job" —or non-verbal tactics such as ignoring a client can be effective with regard to keeping the client in a position of relying on the professional for approval.

Communication of mixed-messages:

For example, calling the client and telling him or her how important it is that (s)he attend his or her next therapy appointment, then standing the client up for that appointment.

Deliberate induction of anxiety:

This can have a devastating effect on clients who may be prone to anxiety or panic attacks, or may have separation anxiety or abandonment issues. The professional may threaten to terminate the relationship so as to coercively persuade the client to comply with certain conditions or requests; or "flirt" with someone else over the phone in the presence of the client, so as to make the client feel jealous or fear abandonment.

These tactics are very similar to those used in the process by which prisoners of war are "brainwashed" by their captives and rendered helpless and dependent upon them. In extreme situations, the victim will identify with the aggressor ("Stockholm Syndrome") and commit acts which (s)he would not commit under normal circumstances—usually at the insistence of the professional. An example of this would be the Patty Hearst kidnapping case in 1974 in California wherein Patty Hearst was kidnapped, locked in a small closet for months, and ultimately coercively persuaded by her captors to commit crimes. The Stockholm Syndrome will be described in more detail in a subsequent chapter of this book.

COUNTERTRANSFERENCE PROBLEMS

An important element of the psychotherapy relationship is that of *transference*, whereby the client unconsciously "transfers" feelings and unresolved issues pertaining to significant others in the client's life onto the therapist; the therapist is then used symbolically to help resolve the unfinished business. The flip-side of this is *counter-transference*, which is basically the therapist's reaction to the client's transference. For example, an attractive female client might transfer feelings onto a male therapist which she originally had for her ex-boyfriend; the therapist might in turn have a counter-transference reaction of sexual attraction to the client.

The therapist has a fiduciary duty to his or her clients to refrain from acting-out counter-transference issues, especially where sexual feelings are involved. Acting-out of counter-transference on the part of therapists has an extremely high potential for rendering the psychotherapeutic relationship ineffectual and damaging. Every therapist who is unable to resolve his or her own counter-transference issues with a client has a duty to seek therapy or refer the client to a different therapist.

Case Example: Sexual Abuse by Clinical Psychologist

   *Dr. Harold Smith was a clinical psychologist in *Nevada. His job consisted of developing programs within the county which would focus on the needs of at-risk youth and included administration of diagnostic tests and counseling parents and kids. Dr. Smith also volunteered his services as a consultant to the local police department, and served on a child abuse prevention committee.

   *Carol was a 13-year-old Middle School student on the verge of expulsion for problem behaviors. Carol came from a dysfunctional and abusive family in which both parents lacked appropriate parenting skills. Although Carol's brothers and sisters experienced some occasional difficulties in school, none of them were considered to be problematic students. Carol acted-out by associating with peers who used alcohol and drugs, committed petty crimes such as vandalism, shoplifting, and malicious mischief, was truant from school, got into numerous fights on campus, and ran away from home frequently. She had been on the verge of arrest, many times, and had been advised that continued behavior of this sort would result in incarceration at a Juvenile Detention Facility.

   Carol was referred to Dr. Smith for counseling. Initially, Dr. Smith counseled Carol and her parents; eventually, however, the parents eventually refused to attend counseling, in an attempt to avoid dealing with their own interpersonal issues, stating that Carol had and was causing all of the problems in the home and at school, and that Dr. Smith should "fix" her. Carol resented having to see Dr. Smith and didn't trust him, believing that he would "rat her out" to the school principal and the police if she were to disclose her feelings to him. She had been told by Dr. Smith that if she did not attend counseling she would be placed in a juvenile detention facility. Carol rebelled with further acting-out behaviors, going as far as targeting Dr. Smith's property—e.g., trashing his office, flattening his tires—hoping that he would become angry at her and terminate the counseling sessions. To her disappointment, that did not happen.

Dr. Smith began grooming Carol by telling her that he intended to keep seeing her because he cared about her and did not want her to go to the juvenile detention facility. He attempted to gain her trust by telling her that he could keep the police off her back if she was cooperative with him in counseling. He told her that she could feel free to talk to him anytime she wanted to, and that rather than cutting classes at school she should simply request to see Dr. Smith during class time. This way, absences could be verified and excused by the school's attendance clerk, and Carol would not be reported as truant. Dr. Smith's office was within walking distance from Carol's school. Carol began to test Dr. Smith by disclosing insignificant incidents, to see whether Dr. Smith would report these incidents to the principal or the police. When it appeared to Carol that Dr. Smith was in fact trustworthy, she began to trust him with more pertinent emotional and behavioral matters.

At the same time Dr. Smith was working on gaining Carol's trust, unbeknownst to her he was also grooming his colleagues and setting up his defense: that Carol was "mentally ill." Dr. Smith made disparaging comments about Carol to her teachers, school counselor, and the principal—e.g., that Carol was a liar and a dope addict and should not be trusted. Dr. Smith explained to Carol that her behavior problems had a diagnosis called "psychosis". He encouraged Carol to explain to her teachers that the psychosis was the cause of her acting-out. Whenever Carol's teachers would confront her about her behavior or truancy, Carol followed Dr. Smith's advice and explained that she acted that way because of a psychosis. Carol's teachers would then consult with Dr. Smith about what they had been told, and Dr. Smith would deny having made that diagnosis. Teachers and school administration were convinced that Carol could not be believed under any circumstances—just as Dr. Smith had forewarned them. This was exactly what Dr. Smith intended to have happen.

Dr. Smith began making seemingly insignificant physical contacts with Carol—e.g., putting his arm around her shoulders, patting her on the back—as well as increased verbal compliments and flirting—e.g., "You look pretty, today," or, "You are a very attractive young lady." Dr. Smith took advantage of Carol's vulnerability in that he knew she didn't receive much in the way of compliments or affection at home. He also began scheduling her weekly sessions at his private office during times when he knew that his receptionist would be away on her lunch break or running errands.

Dr. Smith finally initiated sexual contact with Carol under the pretext of a hypnosis session, telling her that she was "too uptight" and "needed to learn to relax" and that he would show her "a better way to get high without using drugs." He told Carol that he wanted to have sex with her because she was "special" to him. He continued to sexually abuse Carol at his office at least twice per week during that school semester. He justified the frequent sessions to the staff at Carol's school by saying that he was administering batteries of tests, counseling, etc. Nobody bothered to question this. Nor did anybody bother to inquire as to Dr. Smith's counseling notes or test results summaries—neither of which existed. In fact, had anybody looked in Dr. Smith's desk drawers and file cabinet, they would have discovered his pornography collection which included pictures of teenaged girls.

During one session, after sexually abusing Carol, Dr. Smith reportedly made some disparaging comments to her. Carol responded with a barrage of profanity and left, slamming the office door. Unbeknownst to Carol and Dr. Smith, another psychologist,

*Dr. Frank Davis, was in the office downstairs from Dr. Smith's during Carol's "counseling session." Dr. Davis was aware that the conversation in Dr. Smith's office had stopped, and that Dr. Smith and his client continued to remain in the office for a long period of time. When Dr. Davis heard the slamming door and Carol yelling profanity, Dr. Davis went to Dr. Smith's office and inquired as to what had happened in there. Dr. Smith responded that they had a therapy session. Dr. Davis confronted Dr. Smith with his suspicions about the sexual abuse. Dr. Smith initially denied everything, but eventually admitted to the abuse when confronted with evidence. Dr. Davis told him that if it ever happened again and he found out about it he would report Dr. Smith to the police. At that time, there were no mandatory reporting laws pertaining to suspected child sexual abuse. (Present laws provide for criminal penalties for failure to report actual or suspected abuse cases.) Dr. Davis informed Carol that he knew about the sexual situation between her and Dr. Smith. Carol confronted Dr. Smith and asked him why he hadn't told her that Dr. Davis had found out about their relationship. Dr. Smith responded that he didn't tell Carol because he didn't want her to have to carry that with her for the rest of her life. *How 'considerate' of him! Never mind that she would have to carry around the effects of his sexual abuse for the rest of her life...!*

Dr. Davis eventually took a job at a hospital in another state and Dr. Smith resumed sexual contact with Carol, after again playing on her vulnerability and convincing her that he cared about and loved her, and that Dr. Davis was the "bad guy" for breaking their relationship apart. In fact, Dr. Smith used the situation as an example of the reason it was crucial that nobody discover their relationship: if anybody were to find out, they would break it up. Dr. Smith instilled a false sense of guilt in Carol so as to ensure secrecy by telling her that, if he got caught having sex with a teenager, he would never be allowed to work with kids, again. He told her that he would be out pumping gas or mopping floors. Carol, most likely, would end up becoming a ward of the court. Therefore, it was Carol's "responsibility" to keep the relationship a secret. Carol did her utmost to protect Dr. Smith.

Carol resumed using drugs, dropped out of school, and worked as a prostitute while still a minor. The sexual abuse by Dr. Smith continued until she was 21 years old. She did not realize, during the years that she was involved with Dr. Smith, that she was a victim of sexual abuse. She was of the impression that she and Dr. Smith had a genuine, loving relationship. It wasn't until Carol sought therapy from a different psychotherapist that she was able to acknowledge that Dr. Smith's conduct was in fact sexual abuse. After several years of therapy, and upon realizing that Dr. Smith probably had other victims based on a statement that he repeatedly made to her over the years about having a particular sexual attraction to teenaged girls, she decided to report Dr. Smith to the police and sue him for damages.

Carol's therapist's attempt to report Dr. Smith to the police was described in the Prologue of this book. The police never investigated Carol's case. However, with the help of a competent attorney, Carol was able to obtain an out-of-court settlement for civil damages. The problem with Carol's case was that, since the abuse was ongoing for so many years, the statute of limitations within which to initiate legal action had expired by the time Carol reported the abuse. The expiration of the statute of limitations was advantageous to Dr. Smith. He was able to continue working in his capacity of clinical psychologist. Dr. Smith was never required to obtain psychological treatment for his sexual preferences for teenagers; nor was he ever required to register as a sex offender, since he was never arrested for, or convicted of, his crimes. As of this date, Dr. Smith either continues to work in private practice or for a public agency. Carol, on the other hand, suffered from severe, chronic depression, which affected her ability to live a normal life. She dropped out of high school and college and, due to her chronic depression, had to retain the services of a State Vocational rehabilitation agency in order to find and keep employment.

Subsequent to Carol's lawsuit, Dr. Smith contacted Carol by phone and expressed anger and shock at her for disclosing their "relationship" to her therapist and seeking damages, stating that the process was "very painful" for him. He attempted to persuade her that she should reimburse him for the amount of the settlement. As is typical of many child molesters, Dr. Smith was in total denial of having done anything wrong, and expressed no remorse for the pain which he caused Carol during the years the abuse occurred, or the pain which she would continue to experience for the rest of her life.

SCHOOL PSYCHOLOGISTS AND COUNSELORS

School psychologists and counselors are not therapists per se, but function in positions pertaining to academic placement and achievement. Much of their work is conducted so as to meet the needs of Special Education students. With regard to school psychologists, the National Association of School Psychologists is the entity responsible for establishment of ethical standards. Many school psychologists are not licensed to conduct psychotherapy, while others might hold masters or doctorate degrees in counseling or clinical psychology and a State license to operate an independent private psychotherapy practice. Typically, most school psychologists and counselors have completed a Masters degree and have been issued a State credential which authorizes them to be employed in public schools, usually at the kindergarten through twelfth grade levels. Depending upon the policy of the individual school districts, school psychologists and counselors may have an obligation to refer students whom they believe need therapy to outside therapists, so as to avoid conflicts of interest and dual roles.

School psychologists have a duty to provide services which are in the best interests of their students. The *Professional Conduct Manual Principles for Professional Ethics Guidelines for the Provision of School Psychological Services* (Professional Standards Revision Committee; National Association of School Psychologists, 2000), states the following with regard to professional competency:

> "School psychologists recognize the strengths and limitations of their training and experience, engaging only in practices for which they are qualified. They enlist the assistance of other specialists in supervisory, consultative, or referral roles as appropriate in providing services."

> "School psychologists refrain from any activity in which their personal problems or conflicts may interfere with professional effectiveness. Competent assistance is sought to alleviate conflicts in professional relationships."

> "School psychologists are committed to the application of their professional expertise for the purpose of promoting improvement in the quality of life for children, their families, and the school community. This objective is pursued in ways that protect the dignity and rights of those involved."

> "School psychologists do not exploit clients through professional relationships or condone these actions in their colleagues. No individuals, including children, clients, employees, colleagues, trainees, parents, supervisees, and research participants will be exposed to deliberate comments, gestures, or physical contacts of a sexual nature. School psychologists do not harass or demean others based on personal

characteristics. School psychologists do not engage in sexual relationships with their students, supervisees, trainees, or past or present clients."

[Copyright 2000 by the National Association of School Psychologists, Bethesda, MD. Use of this material is by permission of the publisher. www.nasponline.org]

Case Example: School Psychologist

*Dr. Jack Elliot was a school psychologist in his early thirties. He had been employed by the same school district for a number of years and was engaged to be married the year that he seduced and sexually abused a male high school student.

The student, a high school sophomore named *Adam, came from a severely dysfunctional family. He had been referred to Dr. Elliot because, during a routine search of students' lockers, school administrators found his personal journal in which he described feelings of depression and had outlined a suicide plan in detail. Adam had made several suicide gestures on previous occasions, and was considered to be a troublesome student. Adam was highly gifted, according to intelligence tests, but was underachieving and failing nearly all of his classes. Adam's parents were professionals in the community who had recently divorced. Each parent blamed the other for their son's emotional problems. Adam's mother was very narcissistic and refused to acknowledge that her son needed professional help. She occasionally teased him about feeling suicidal, and constantly threatened to send him to live with his father if he didn't "start behaving himself." Adam did not want to live with his father because the man had a bad temper and was physically abusive. Neither parent wanted to be identified as the "parent of a special ed student."

Adam was cooperative with Dr. Elliot in counseling sessions. He believed that Dr. Elliot was there to help him. Dr. Elliot played on Adam's need for a father-figure, taking him to football games, movies, and other outings. Sometimes, Dr. Elliot had Adam spend the night at his house. At some point, Dr. Elliot began showing Adam pornographic magazines during counseling sessions. Elliot would tell Adam to lock the office door, or hang the "TESTING IN PROGRESS, DO NOT DISTURB" sign on the outside doorknob. Dr. Elliot would move his chair closer to Adam, or both of them would sit on the office floor, while they looked at the magazines. During one session, Dr. Elliot pulled his pants down and masturbated in front of Adam. At the next session, he encouraged Adam to do likewise, and had Adam perform fellatio on him. The sexual abuse continued for the duration of Adam's high school enrollment. Adam did not perceive the relationship as sexual abuse, although he knew that he couldn't tell anybody about it as that would get Dr. Elliot into trouble. Ironically, the abuse occurred in Dr. Elliot's office which was located in the Administration building at the high school. There was continuous student and faculty foot traffic down the hallway directly outside the office. The Principal's office was just three doors down the same hallway.

Dr. Elliot had a duty to place Adam in a special education class for the Seriously Emotionally Disturbed, because Adam was a gifted student who could not learn or progress academically because of the chronic depression which he experienced. Dr. Elliot did not place Adam in the SED class because he knew that placing Adam in that type of program would eventually enable Adam to recover from the depression and realize that he had been the victim of sexual abuse. Dr. Elliot relied on Adam's dependency on him; as long as Adam remained chronically depressed and perceived him as a "friend," the more likely that Adam would keep the abuse a secret. Adam met the criteria as a disabled student who, **by law**, was entitled to receive accommodations, modifications, and whatever else it would have required to assist him with learning and progressing academically. Dr. Elliot, in effect, illegally discriminated against Adam by his failure to place him in the Special Education class.

Adam sought psychotherapy from a psychiatrist a few years later and was given anti-depressive medications. In therapy, he discussed the "relationship" that he had been having with Dr. Elliot. The psychiatrist helped Adam to acknowledge that Dr. Elliot's behavior was a crime, and empowered him to report Dr. Elliot to the State Credentialing agency. Adam also filed a lawsuit against Dr. Elliot for malpractice. Unfortunately, by the time the complaint was filed, the statute of limitations had elapsed and the case was settled out of court for a nominal amount of money. After calculating the math in terms of the settlement amount— the total amount divided by the number of years, weeks, and days that Adam was subjected to abuse—Adam commented that the settlement amounted to less than minimum wage. It constituted a slap on the wrist for Dr. Elliot, who was able to keep his job at the school district without ever having to register as a sex offender.

* * * * * * * * * *

PSYCHOTHERAPISTS AS INTERN SUPERVISORS

Most states require students in graduate-level counseling and psychology programs to complete an internship, prior and subsequent to graduation, consisting of a specified number of hours ranging from 1000 to 3000, in order to become eligible to take the State Licensing Examination. These interns must be supervised by therapists who have been licensed for a minimum number of years.

It is unethical and even illegal in some states for supervisors to become sexually involved with their interns. However, an issue arises as to consensual relationships between the intern and supervisor. The appropriate action in these cases is for the supervisor to terminate the internship, since the sexual relationship will no doubt render the supervisor less effective in the performance of his/her duties.

Another issue arises with regard to sexual harassment in the workplace when supervisors adopt a quid pro quo type of policy whereby the intern is expected to exchange sexual favors as payment for supervision and completion of the required internship hours. This practice is illegal and supervisors who engage in it may be held liable for discrimination and Labor Code violations.

PSYCHOTHERAPISTS AS COLLEGE PROFESSORS

Similar ethical issues exist with regard to psychotherapists who are also college professors. Each college and university may have its own policy regarding consensual relationships between students and professors. Some institutions might permit these relationships under certain conditions, while others strictly forbid them.

When professors expect students to exchange sexual favors for high or passing grades, an ethical line is definitely crossed. Professors who sexually harass students set themselves up for legal consequences, as this conduct constitutes unlawful discrimination.

Types of harassment typically prohibited by college campuses include unwelcome and unsolicited conduct meeting the following criteria when directed to an individual's gender, sexual orientation, race, color, religion, marital status, national origin, ancestry, disability, or any other protected classification:

Physical: stalking, unwanted touching;
Verbal: sexual jokes, obscene phone calls, slurs;
Visual: graffiti, posters, email, letters, derogatory symbols, pornographic magazines;

Case Example: Dr. James Nivette, College Professor
and Clinical Psychologist

James Nivette was a California college professor and clinical psychologist who had been in practice for at least 20 years. Additionally, he was a reserve police officer, and consultant to police and Sheriff's departments throughout his county of residence. He was also a power-tripper obsessed with guns. Court records state that Nivette often threatened his girlfriends at gunpoint into compliance with his requests.

Nivette had a reputation for seducing female clients and students, particularly targeting those who were emotionally needy with low self-esteem. He was notorious for his empty promises and lies. One of his tall tales consisted of him as a former Air Force pilot and POW in Vietnam. Another portrayed him as a duke from another country. Yet in another, he was a spy for a United States government agency. He told his victims that his wife had died in a skiing accident in Switzerland. Unbeknownst to the victims, Nivette was still legally married to her, and she was alive and well and living in California. Several of his victims describe him as an expert in playing psychological "mind games" and brainwashing. He would reinforce his victims' dependency on him and exploit their fears of abandonment and rejection. Victims describe how they would arrive at Nivette's home, school office, or private office on numerous occasions for scheduled appointments and discover him having sex with other women. This was one of the "mind games" deliberately pre-arranged by Nivette so as to make all of the women involved jealous of each other, as he had told each of them that she was his "one and only." Nivette also used his authority as a psychologist to the detriment of others. On one occasion, Nivette had one of his victims confined for a 72-hour observation in a mental health unit of a local hospital subsequent to beating her up, alleging that she was a danger to herself and others. This was an attempt on his part to destroy her credibility in the event that she decided to press charges against him.

The California Board of Psychology revoked Nivette's license to practice psychotherapy in 1995 as the result of a lawsuit filed by one of his clients whom he sexually abused. This particular client initially sought marriage counseling from Nivette. However, Nivette seduced her and maintained a five-year affair with her whereby they would have sex on a weekly basis at his office. The client sustained an unwanted pregnancy, had an abortion, and eventually divorced her husband.

Nivette had a history of multiple arrests for domestic violence against his wife. In order to avoid prosecution, he would persuade her via the usual apologies, sweet talk, and empty promises, as is typical in domestic violence cases, to drop the charges. Nivette's wife obtained a restraining order against Nivette in 1995 due to the fact that he owned numerous guns and she feared for her safety. She filed for divorce in 1995.

Nivette met 20-year-old Gina Barnett in traffic school in 1995, became sexually involved with her, and was arrested and convicted for misdemeanor assault when he beat her up at her apartment. As a condition of his probation, Nivette was not allowed to possess guns of any type. However, Nivette managed to convince the judge that he used guns only for target practice, and the restriction was lifted. On November 18, 1997, Nivette murdered Barnett by repeatedly shooting her as she was running up the stairs of their residence in an attempt to escape from him. He abandoned their 18-month-old son on a sidewalk near the San Francisco Airport. The boy was rescued and Barnett's mother was given custody of him. All of this occurred while Nivette was still on probation for the aforementioned domestic violence incident. Nivette immediately left for France where he lived at his residence in Munster for four years.

Approximately four years after being apprehended and incarcerated by officials in France, Nivette was extradited to Sacramento, California, on the condition that United States officials would not seek the death penalty against him. At that time, however, Nivette's crime was not one which called for the death penalty. The judge sentenced Nivette to 18 years to life in prison for the murder of Barnett. At his sentencing hearing in 2004, a letter from his 7-year-old son was read to the court by Deputy District Attorney Frank Meyer, which stated: "I never got to meet my mom because my dad, James Nivette, killed her. I hope he stays in prison until he dies."

TERRI AUSTIN, PH.D., J.D.

NOTES:

Notes:

CHAPTER FOUR:

ABUSE BY PRIESTS

In the summer of 2005, I attended a peaceful demonstration outside St. Mary's Cathedral in San Francisco conducted by an organization known as SNAP (Survivors Network of those Abused by Priests). Survivors of abuse wore t-shirts which said "Stop the Cover-Up!" and carried posters which depicted photographs of themselves as children or teenagers at the age which they were molested by a trusted member of the clergy. SNAP directors and survivors from all over California participated in this demonstration. Archbishop William Levada was to officiate his final mass at the Cathedral prior to leaving for Rome to assume his new assignment as Cardinal. Before mass started, he was served with a subpoena ordering him to appear at a deposition to give testimony as to his role in sexual abuse cover-ups over the years. Levada initially refused to accept the subpoena. However, when given the option of accepting the subpoena voluntarily right then and there, or being forced to accept it during the mass when process servers would rush the altar, Levada decided on the former. He commented that the service of process was a "disgrace to the church." The process server responded, "No—YOU are a disgrace to the church."

In January, 2006, when Cardinal Levada arrived in San Francisco for the deposition, SNAP members held a vigil outside of the attorney's office at which the deposition was scheduled to take place. A process server had in his possession a subpoena compelling Levada to attend yet another deposition pertaining to his role in more sexual abuse cover-ups in another State. While awaiting Levada's arrival, SNAP members talked to news media and handed out leaflets to the public which explained Levada's role as a key figure in the church sexual abuse cover-up. The leaflets also described SNAP's requests to Cardinal Levada with regard to helping protect children by listing all of the names of known or accused clergy sex offenders on an international website, and to expedite the process of defrocking molesters. It has been estimated that approximately fewer than one-hundred of five-thousand American clerics who have been accused of sexual abuse have actually been defrocked.

A few minutes prior to the scheduled time for the deposition, Cardinal WIlliam Levada, the highest-ranking American official at the Vatican, evidently lacking the courage to face the SNAP group, was seen exiting his vehicle around the back of the building, attempting to sneak in via the delivery entrance like a criminal in hiding. The process server wasted no time in handing him the subpoena.

Levada, in his position as Archbishop, was notorious for transfering numerous predator priests to different parishes, allowing them to remain in their positions as priests with unrestricted access to children. He has also refused to reveal identities of accused child molester clergy; and he has retaliated against accusers and whistle-blowers. For all practical and legal purposes, this makes him an accessory to the crimes.

Levada is only one of many significant players in the Catholic church sexual abuse cover-up game.

* * * * * * * * *

THE CHURCH SEXUAL ABUSE SCANDAL

The focus of this chapter will be on sexual offenses committed by Catholic priests. Although sexual abuse is committed by clergy in other denominations, statistics indicate that the problem is more prevalent within the Catholic church. At the time of this writing, research indicates that there are presently over 4500 Catholic priests in the United States who have sexually abused at least 10,000 children since approximately the 1950's. These calculations most likely are a representation of only the tip of the proverbial iceberg.

Sex offender priests do not seem to differ significantly from other child molesters. Many of them have similar narcissistic and antisocial traits, prior sex offenses, and deviant sexual interests. However, as is consistent with other professionals, the sex offender priests have a higher level of education than non-clergy offenders or those who are not employed in a professional capacity.

Sexual abuse of children and young adults by priests has been ongoing since at least approximately the 1500's. Pope Julius III reportedly had a long-term affair with a 15-year-old boy whom he eventually ordained a cardinal. It is only within the past couple of decades that the sexual abuse incidents and cover-ups have been surfacing, as victims have acquired the courage to speak out about their abuse. Initially, people were resistant to the idea that priests are capable of committing terrible crimes such as rape, child sexual abuse, and even murder. The public believed that priests could do no wrong, and attorneys and law enforcement officials were reluctant to become involved in the investigation and prosecution of priests as child molesters. Some police departments had an "unwritten rule" that members of the clergy were not to be arrested. Instead, victims were blamed, stonewalled, and accused of lying; and priests who were sexual perpetrators simply transferred to different parishes without any disclosure made to parishioners about the priests' prior conduct. In the 1980's a canon attorney, Reverend Thomas Doyle, submitted the first written report to the bishops of the United States about the large number of sexual offender clergy. At that time, no action was taken.

Cardinal Levada, formerly Archbishop of the San Francisco Archdiocese, replaced Cardinal Ratzinger upon Ratzinger's becoming Pope Benedict XVI. In his newly-appointed position in

Rome, Levada's job duties include investigation of allegations of sexual abuse by priests and other employees of the church. Apparently, Levada was selected by Pope Benedict for this position as Cardinal based on their friendship and previously having worked together. Levada does not have the appropriate qualifications or credentials to investigate suspected sexual abuse incidents and other inappropriate conduct. In fact, ironically, Levada utilized a canon lawyer priest, whom he knew was indicted for sexual abuse of a minor, as his legal expert on issues pertaining to the church sexual abuse crisis. Levada has been well-aware of this priest's conduct for at least the past decade.

PSYCHOLOGICAL ISSUES OF CATHOLIC PRIESTS

Arrested Development

Most men become priests because they have a genuine desire to help people and be positive contributors to parishes and their community. Others are attracted to the profession for different reasons including those originating in psychopathology and emotional and mental instability.

A career in the priesthood offers job security, housing, benefits, and a steady income. Authority is an inherent feature of the collar and clerical uniform, and is based on the priest having an allegedly privileged "connection," of some sort, with God. Other perks of the job include household and office services such as secretarial, housekeeping, gardening, janitorial, and maintenance. Most priests do not have to do their own cooking or laundry. Accompanying the job security is the assurance that one will not have to apply for and possibly face rejection from, "regular" jobs in the civilian community. The need to stand in unemployment or welfare lines is eliminated, and it is not necessary to start at the bottom of the proverbial workplace ladder and work one's way up, since "promotions" seem to be based on knowing the right people in the church Administration. Promotions are also contingent upon priests' ability to appear to keep a lid on problems occurring within their parishes. The *appearance* of a nice, quiet, chaos-free parish infers that the priest or pastor is doing an effective job even when that might not necessarily be the case.

Most seminary students enroll in the seminary immediately upon attaining a bachelor's degree, and are typically in their early 20's. They have not been married or involved in long-term healthy relationships, nor had the opportunity to experience life fully as young adults. Needless to say, many of these young men are struggling with personal and sexual identity issues. Arrested sexual development is an issue with priests because they typically are discouraged from developing emotionally and psycho-sexually and, as a result, many tend to function as young teenaged boys in adult male bodies.

This factor would make certain priests susceptible to pursuing relationships with children or teenagers whom they consider their "peers" and to whom they feel they can relate on an emotional level.

It has been said that priests are selfless people. This tends to be true—since the profession allows very little time for oneself due to the requirement that priests always be available to other people. The Church's expectation that a psychologically and emotionally immature young man is capable of making the decision to remain celibate for the remainder of his entire life, in commitment to a religious organization, is a very unrealistic one. Most young adults in their twenties are uncertain as to their commitments for the upcoming year, let alone the rest of their lives.

Personality Disorders

Priests with Antisocial tendencies and who are high-functioning are in a position whereby successful deception of the public is possible. These individuals know that the faithful are very highly unlikely to doubt or question words coming from a priest. It can be a relatively simple process to scam people out of money and property in the name of all that is holy. Realistically, individuals with a full-blown Antisocial Personality Disorder who are low-functioning are not found in the clergy, since they lack self-discipline and have a tendency to engage in conduct which frequently and consistently results in arrest and incarceration. Chances are that they would not be able to stay out of prison long enough to pursue any type of a career, let alone a religious one.

Narcissistic priests are in an ideal situation for fulfilling their insatiable needs for admiration and attaining their unrealistic expectations of entitlement and favorable treatment. The church setting is the ideal forum to act-out grandiose beliefs of self-importance and power. People are always at their beck and call, and ultimately disposal. The narcissistic priest, through his position of authority, preys on the vulnerable and suggestible for the purpose of bolstering his own fragile ego. This particular priest literally "plays God" on a vicarious basis, in order to over-compensate for feelings of inferiority. The religious vestments serve as a cover-up for his deep-seated insecurities and inadequacies. Behavior which outwardly appears to be self-sacrificing and caring is only for the purpose of projecting a favorable impression on the public. In other words, most of it is a big show. The narcissistic priest cannot survive without the positive regard, admiration, and attention of his parishioners. He will make disparaging remarks about his parishioners behind their backs; and he will simultaneously justify his association with them in terms of "having to do (his) job". The narcissistic priest is incapable of establishing genuine, caring relationships with others. His main pursuit is the feeding of his own ego and, in the process, he doesn't care who gets hurt. He is an expert at exploitation and will not hesitate to exploit his congregation and colleagues.

Since narcissists have difficulty with emotions—their own and others'—the priesthood offers a lifestyle within which it is possible to run from, deny, suppress, and repress one's emotions and true self. The celibacy requirement, for those who abide by it, may actually serve as a convenience to the narcissistic priest because the requirement, in a sense, allows him to have his cake and eat it, too, with regard to intimate relationships. The priest who dates someone on a regular basis—whether that person is of the same or opposite sex—has the advantage of being able to hide behind the vestments the instant he perceives conflict in a relationship. In most cases, the conflict usually arises from the priest's own inconsiderate conduct, although he will never admit to this. He simply blows a lot of smoke and then hides behind the smokescreen until he thinks that the conflict has resolved itself. Then, he will act as though nothing ever happened.

Narcissistic men—including narcissistic priests—hate and fear women. Women have emotions and needs, neither of which the narcissist is able to deal with. Women, especially beautiful ones, are often used as "arm candy" and discarded once they have outlived their usefulness.

Case Example: *Father Fred Maxwell: Master Manipulator*

*Fred Maxwell enrolled in a *New York seminary while in his late teens—one which has a reputation for a predominantly gay environment—and was ordained to the priesthood while in his early twenties. Maxwell, by his own admission, came very close to being expelled from the seminary on a few occasions, but was able to avoid this by "playing their game so they wouldn't throw (Maxwell) out." Subsequent to graduation from the seminary, Maxwell was assigned to a parish. He reportedly bragged about becoming involved in an affair with a young female employee of the diocese, named *Shirley. Maxwell was also in charge of the Youth Ministry program of the parish whereby he would coordinate recreational activities for the parish teenagers, including weekend retreats, pizza parties, movie outings, and fundraisers. Maxwell and another priest accompanied the teenagers to the weekend retreats. Shirley would also participate in the youth retreats at Maxwell's insistence, and Maxwell claims to have had have sex with her in the office of the retreat facility, while the other priest kept the teenagers occupied with other projects. This relationship was short-lived. Shirley terminated it upon realizing that Maxwell made numerous empty promises, and could not be trusted. In retaliation, Maxwell spread malicious and lies and gossip about Shirley, in an attempt to protect his own reputation. Maxwell was transferred to another parish where he was again placed in charge of the Youth Ministry activities, including promoting priestly vocations to young men. Maxwell developed close friendships with a few families in the new parish, many of whom had teenagers.

Maxwell's conduct met the criteria for Narcissistic Personality Disorder. He also had hypo-manic and paranoid tendencies, smoked marijuana and used alcohol on a consistently regular basis. He came across as intelligent, "cool", rebellious, and tough. Underneath all of this, he was an extremely confused and insecure person. He had a rapport with teenagers and, on one occasion when pulled over by the police for a speeding violation, claims to have impressed a carload of his teenaged passengers by talking his way out of a speeding ticket. He simply told the patrol officer that he was on his way to the hospital to administer last rites to a critically ill patient. Maxwell had an obsession with power and control, and was skilled in manipulating others for his own benefits. Maxwell was also chaplain to a local police department, which gave him police reserve officer status. He provided marijuana and alcohol to teenagers and to his friends, bragging about how his position as police chaplain gave him access to information and sources for street drugs. He was known to brag about tapping into the church collection money so as to fund his marijuana and liquor habits while blaming altar boys or the music ministry for the missing money.

Maxwell resided at the parish rectory but had a separate apartment which he maintained with another young man, which was often the site for parties. Maxwell eventually gave up his apartment at the insistence of the Diocese. At some point, the Bishop of Maxwell's diocese placed a priest in Maxwell's rectory who reportedly was "dirty from another diocese." Maxwell was designated to "baby-sit" the priest for the few months that the priest was to stay at the parish. Parishioners were told that the new priest was an "assistant" and not a word was said about the fact that he had been transferred to the parish because of his behavioral problems in the other diocese.

Maxwell was transferred to yet another parish where, contrary to the diocese's wishes, he occasionally would have runaway boys and male street hustlers spend the night in the rectory, disregarding the protests and complaints of rectory staff. Maxwell provided alcohol and marijuana to these teenaged boys. He also provided and viewed pornographic videos and magazines with them, and took the boys to nudist beaches, justifying these excursions as "educational."

Maxwell was aware that the Diocese had been questioning his sexual inclinations and mental health ever since his ordination. In order to deflect the Diocese's concerns about his possible sexual orientation, Maxwell began dating a young female college student from another town, whom he had known for a number of years. The young woman—*Katie—was a child sexual abuse survivor and still vulnerable from the effects of the abuse. Maxwell was very much aware of Katie's previous abuse and state of vulnerability. He told her that he was in the process of quitting his job as a priest because of constant conflicts between himself and the diocese. The relationship was of a platonic nature and consisted primarily of Maxwell taking her to dinner at fancy restaurants, movies, and concerts every couple of weeks. Maxwell would often put his arm around Katie in public, and appear to be affectionate with her. Unbeknownst to Katie, she was merely "arm candy" and his seemingly affectionate behavior was a big show so as to keep the diocese off his back about his suspected sexual orientation—a fact which she would not discover until fifteen years later. Maxwell was initially every bit the gentleman in the relationship—opening doors for her, buying her flowers and candy, sending numerous "I love you" cards and letters, and displaying physical affection. He constantly told her how much he looked forward to seeing her and, eventually persuaded her to give him a key to her apartment, so that he could go there "to take a nap and get away from the craziness at the rectory." (A couple of years later, Katie discovered that he was using her apartment for other purposes). He told her that he had very strong feelings for her ever since she was a teenager and, once he quit his job, wanted to make a commitment to her. He cautioned her that it was crucial that she not disclose this to anyone, because if the diocese were to find out about his "future plans" the diocese had the power to interfere with those plans. Katie took him at his word—after all, he was a priest, and supposedly a trustworthy, longtime friend.

Maxwell led Katie on for approximately two years. Whenever Katie inquired as to the process of his resignation from his job, he would tell her that it was "going slow" and blamed church officials for the delay. At one point when Katie demanded to see copies of the "papers" pertaining to terminating his job, which

Maxwell claimed to be filing at the Cardinal's office, Maxwell accused Katie of being "bitchy", "needy", pushy, and having unrealistic expectations. His attitude toward her changed and he began to criticize her, becoming verbally abusive, and threatening to abandon her. Unbeknownst to her, he made disparaging and defamatory comments about her to his male friends and rectory staff. He disclosed information to his friends, which Katie had told him in confidence, about Katie's past history of sexual abuse. Katie never consented to this disclosure. When Katie discovered this breach of confidentiality and confronted Maxwell, he denied any knowledge of how people obtained the information. After being harassed at her residence by some of Maxwell's friends, Katie called the police. When questioned, Maxwell told police that Katie was stalking him and made other false statements about her. Maxwell would later call Katie and reassure her that he loved and cared about her, and caution her that she was not to disclose anything to the police about their relationship. Although police were helpful, they were very reluctant to prosecute a priest or hold the Church responsible for Maxwell's conduct, as the situation appeared to be more of a civil as opposed to criminal matter. Katie discontinued contact with Maxwell, realizing that his problems were unlikely to go away on their own, and that he would only cause her further pain. Maxwell was eventually transferred to another parish located a significant distance from where Katie resided.

Katie was later informed by an attorney and former employees of the administrative offices of Maxwell's diocese that the church Administration had been questioning Maxwell's mental health and sexual inclinations for many, many years, ever since his ordination as a priest, and particularly when they learned about teenaged boys spending the night at the rectory and at Maxwell's apartment. Apparently, Maxwell had a reputation amongst the diocese staff for using people as pawns for his own advantage, lying, threatening others when he couldn't have his own way, and justifying his behavior as morally or legally correct despite intellectual knowledge to the contrary. He was clever at deflecting police investigation into his own conduct.

Maxwell reportedly accused yet another woman, with whom he had been spending time for appearances sake for several months, of "stalking" behaviors. It was discovered that the woman was a lesbian not interested in "stalking" Maxwell or any other man.

The diocese never bothered to investigate their suspicions or the circumstantial evidence which pointed to the possibility that Maxwell might have been sexually abusing teenagers.

Case Example: Father Robert Stevens: Sexual Abuse of A Young Adult

*Father Robert Stevens, a seminary supervisor, preyed on young candidates for the priesthood who were reliant on him for their success in the seminary.

*Javier, a parishioner interested in becoming a priest, sought spiritual counseling from Stevens regarding family problems. Stevens seduced and sexually abused Javier one evening during a counseling session. The "relationship" continued for approximately fifteen years, during which time Stevens impressed upon Javier that the relationship was not in any way wrong. Javier believed him. After a few years, Javier decided that he wanted to become a priest. Once Javier enrolled in the seminary, Stevens fabricated a story about the seminary administration having doubts about Javier's suitability for the priesthood. Stevens convinced Javier that he had the power to persuade them otherwise as long as Javier maintained secrecy about the sexual abuse.

Javier eventually reported the abuse to the Bishop. The Bishop informed him that the behavior was inappropriate—but not abusive—since the relationship was consensual between two adults. The Bishop did not disclose the abuse to the Diocesan Review

Board, as would have been proper procedure in sexual abuse cases. He justified this failure to disclose by stating that the purpose of the Review Board was to investigate allegations of abuse against *children*. Stevens was never disciplined and remained in his position as a priest.

Javier resigned from the priesthood after acknowledging that his unconscious reason for becoming a priest was Stevens's influence over him. (This type of identification with an abuser is characteristic of Stockholm Syndrome, which will be described in a later chapter.) He also realized that he would receive no restitution, support or assistance from the church for having been victimized. To add insult to injury, the Bishop threatened to sue Javier for defamation unless he stopped referring to the situation with Stevens as "sexual abuse."

Sexual Predators and Accomplices to Crime

For years, pedophiles and child molesters employed as priests had a convenient hiding place behind church doors and walls, with the added reassurance that the Church administration will make every attempt to conceal the crimes and enable the offenders to keep their jobs. It seems that, while priests are severely disciplined by church administration for embezzling or misappropriating church funds, they are cut a considerable amount of slack when it comes to child molestation. Apparently, to many religious officials, sexual abuse of children is not as serious an offense as stealing—or being suspected of stealing—the church's money. In a recent Connecticut case, a private investigator was hired to investigate a priest suspected of misappropriating church funds. It was discovered that the priest, Father Michael Fay, drove a jaguar, spent hundreds of thousands of dollars on limousine rides, stayed in the fanciest hotels, bought expensive jewelry, and owned a condominium which he shared with another man. The bishop of the diocese, upon becoming aware of possible embezzlement of funds by Fay, immediately forced Fay to resign. The church has failed to take similar immediate action in sexual abuse cases in many Catholic dioceses.

As of this writing, there exist *over two million five hundred eighty five thousand* articles on the internet which pertain to sexual abuse allegations by priests being consistently denied by the priests, bishops, and Church as a whole so as to protect their reputations. For all practical purposes, bishops and others who cover-up for sexual offender priests should be charged as accomplices to these crimes, in addition to obstruction of justice.

Another issue about which the church is not open is that of priests who have contracted AIDS and who, via their sexual activities, continue to place others at risk for contracting the disease. Since the church is responsible for priests' medical insurance and expenses, it cannot deny knowledge of priest who have AIDS. The bottom line is that past and potential future victims of sexual predator priests—including adults and children—have not been warned about the possible risk and exposure to AIDS. This leaves the public vulnerable to contracting the disease by having sex with persons who are unaware of being carriers of the virus. The church should be held liable to victims who have contracted AIDS as the result of sexual abuse by priests who have AIDS

Case Example: Father John Geoghan

Geoghan, ordained to the priesthood in 1962, worked as a priest in the Boston Archdiocese from 1962-1993. Geoghan had been molesting young boys in at least a half a dozen parishes for decades. Church administration, despite having been informed about Geoghan's conduct, simply transferred him to different parishes where he was allowed to continue interacting with children on a daily basis. Court records indicate that in 1984 Geoghan's sexually abusive behavior was brought to the attention of Cardinal Bernard Law, who later testified in court—under oath—that he had no knowledge of the fact, nor reason to suspect, that Geoghan was a child molester. At least one-hundred-fifty victims claimed to have been sexually abused by Geoghan. The Boston archdiocese initially reneged on a thirty-million dollar settlement with the victims; however, in 2002 reached a ten-million dollar settlement with eighty six of them.

Reportedly, Geoghan received inpatient therapy at several sexual abuse treatment facilities, beginning in 1972, including Saint Luke's Institute in Maryland, Southdown Institute in Ontario, and the Institute of Living in Hartford. The Boston archdiocese was responsible for picking up the tab for the cost of all of these treatments. Geohan's psychiatric treatment was administered by physicians who did not specialize or have experience in the treatment of sex offenders

In February, 2002, Geoghan was sentenced to ten years in prison for molesting a ten-year-old boy at a swimming pool at the Waltham Boys and Girls Club. While incarcerated, Geoghan disclosed to other inmates his plans to relocate to South America upon his release so as to resume contacts with children. He was strangled to death at the Souza-Baranowski Correctional Center in Massachusetts by another inmate, Joseph Druce. Druce, severely homophobic, was serving a life sentence for murdering a man who allegedly made a pass at him after picking him up while hitchhiking.

Cardinal Bernard Law resigned from his position as Cardinal in December, 2002. He finally admitted in a deposition that he was in fact aware of Geoghan's sexual abuse of approximately seven young boys in 1984 prior to transfering Goeghan to other parishes. Law's excuse for protecting Geoghan was that he "failed to keep adequate records." During Law's Cardinalship, at least six

hundred victims of sexual abuse by clergy came forward to disclose their situations

* * * * * * * * *

Approximately 32 states have a requirement that persons designated by law as mandated reporters must report suspected incidents of child sexual abuse. These mandated reporters consist of
numerous professionals—e.g., school employees, child care staff,
and physicians. It is important to note that **not all of the states
include "priests" and "clergy" as mandated reporters.** Information
about child abuse of any type which is obtained through confession has been exempted from mandated reporting in some states,
based on the penitent-clergy privileged communications rule.

Unfortunately, since Massachusetts was one of the states
which did not include priests/clergy in their list of mandated
reporters, Cardinal Bernard Law cannot be held criminally liable for not reporting sexual abuse incidents about which he had
knowledge.

Case Example: Cardinal Roger Mahoney

Cardinal Roger Mahoney served as the Bishop of Fresno,
California, from 1975-1980, and Bishop of Stockton, California
in 1980. Since 1985, he has served as the Archbishop of the Los
Angeles Diocese, where numerous sexual abuse incidents have
been coming to the attention of news media.

Rather than expend time and energy into assisting the victims of clergy abuse, Mahoney has channeled that energy into
a big performance for the benefit of his own reputation----spe-
cifically, that of attempting to convince the public that he has
voluntarily implemented a zero-tolerance sexual abuse policy
with regard to clergy in the Diocese of Los Angeles. In reality, Mahoney and the Diocese were compelled to implement the

zero-tolerance policy as a condition of a settlement in a law-suit in 1988. In this lawsuit, sexual abuse victims of Monsignior Michael Harris alleged that the Diocese knew, for many years, about the accusations against Harris, yet looked the other way and took no action to intervene.

In 2002, after being threatened with a grand jury investiga-tion and having been served with subpoenas by the Grand Jury, Mahoney promised to release confidential personnel files of all of the priests under his supervision who have been accused of sexual abuse. Later, reneging on this promise, he claimed that the personnel files were "under confessional seal", knowing full well that the confessional privilege does not extend to priests' personnel files or to priests and their religious supervisors.

Mahoney made a public statement in 1988 to the effect that he "...would never deal with the sex abuse crisis by transferring a priest to another diocese..." However, records indicate that he has transferred numerous priest perpetrators to other parishes, for many years, a large number of whom were his friends. Some of the priests transferred by Mahoney include:

- Father Michael Wempe: The long-haired, motorcy-cle-riding priest who had a reputation among teen-agers as being "cool" admitted to having molested at least 13 teenaged boys over a period of fifteen years since 1972. Wempe selected victims who were kids from dysfunctional families, thereby abusing his position as a priest and betraying the trust placed in him by those families and the community. In February, 2006, Wempe was convicted of one count of child molestation, and in May, 2006, was sen-tenced to three years in prison.

- Father Carl Sutphin: Appointed to the position of

Associate Pastor of the Cathedral of Los Angeles by Mahoney. In 2002, one of his victims publicly protested this assignment and disclosed that, in 1991, Mahoney promised that Sutphin would retire in exchange for the victim's silence. Sutphin had a history of sexually assaulting boys in the 1960's and 1970's.

- Father Carlos Rodriguez: Transferred to a parish in Santa Barbara after it was discovered that he molested a boy in Los Angeles. One victim's family trusted him to the extent that they gave him a key to their home so that he could come and go whenever he pleased. Among other places, he molested his victims on the seminary premises and at his mother's house. He was arrested in 2004 and is presently serving a prison sentence. Mahoney made a false statement to the effect that, at the time of his arrest, the priest's duties did not involve associating with minors.

- Father Michael Baker: Admitted to Mahoney in 1986 that he had been sexually abusing boys. For the following ten years church administrators assigned him to different parishes where he continued to sexually abuse boys. Mahoney is reported to have paid two victims $1.3 million dollars to remain silent about their sexual abuse ordeals when they threatened to sue the diocese.

- Monsignior Richard Loomis: While Loomis was in charge of handling accusations of sexual abuse and other misconduct against priests, one of his victims disclosed that a civil lawsuit against him was pending for sex offenses. Loomis was placed on paid administrative leave from his position as vicar of the clergy.

- Father Oliver O'Grady: Reassigned to different parishes by church administration, after admitting to Mahoney that he had been molesting boys. He was also transferred to other parishes after receiving a negative psychological evaluation.

VATICAN SOLUTIONS

Gay-Bashing

In November, 2005, in an attempt to give the appearance of providing a solution to the Church sexual abuse crisis, the Vatican published an Instruction titled *Concerning the Criteria for the Discernment with Regards to Persons with Homosexual Tendencies in View of Their Admission to the Seminary and to Holy Orders*. This document, in actuality, appears to be a glorified version of gay-bashing. The question posted in the Instruction is whether to deny applicants with "deep-seated homosexual tendencies" admission to seminaries and ultimately the priesthood. The Vatican answers the question by stating that individuals who practice homosexuality cannot be admitted to seminaries or ordained to the priesthood. Nor can anyone who supports the gay community, or presents with "deep-seated homosexual tendencies." The Vatican states that "transitional" homosexuality, as might be the case with arrested development, is a different situation altogether. Individuals with "transitional homosexuality" would be required to "overcome" this at least three years prior to being ordained as a deacon.

The Vatican has set up a strawman—the gay applicant to the seminary. The Vatican's recent mandate to inspect seminaries for evidence of homosexuality and banning gay men from seminaries appears to be another attempt to shift the focus from abusive clergy and church cover-up. Supposedly, "gay priests molest kids." This is a reflection of either fallacious reasoning—or just plain stupidity!—on the Vatican's part. Eliminating gay men from the seminaries would be similar to having the FBI raid high school students' lockers on campus for small amounts of marijuana rather than direct resources and energy into combating the real problem of illegal drug dealing originating from organized drug cartels. The church sexual abuse scandal is no less a form of organized crime. It is organized with respect to the careful, pre-meditated planning involved in the denial, cover-up, and transferring of offender priests by bishops, archbishops, cardinals and other accessories prior to and after-the-fact.

A recent documentary, *Sex Crimes and the Vatican*, aired in October, 2006, disclosed how Pope Benedict led the cover-up of child sexual abuse by priests. Apparently, in or about 2001, the Pope—formerly Cardinal Ratzinger—issued an updated version of a top-secret document titled *Crimin Sollicitationis* which directed bishops worldwide to discourage all parties involved in sexual abuse crimes within the Church to refrain from discussing the abuse. Bishops were required to keep this document in a locked safe at all times. Victims of sexual abuse who were non-compliant with regard to keeping silent were to be threatened with ex-communication from the Church, as per *Crimin Sollicitationis*.

Screening of applicants to the seminary should attempt to identify and eliminate individuals who are most likely to misuse their power to exploit vulnerable children and adults for their own purpose. Individuals with severe narcissistic or antisocial personality disorders who believe that laws and ethics apply to everyone except themselves should be prohibited from entering the seminaries.

Research has shown that recidivism among preferential child molesters is 100%, as this behavior is extremely difficult if not impossible to cure. Since the mindset of a child molester is identical to that of the serial killer, it is disturbing to think that these types of individuals are knowingly placed in positions of power and trust in our churches. There is no evidence indicating that gay people are more prone to child molesting or serial murder than non-homosexuals. The Vatican's implication that the clergy abuse problem can be solved by eliminating gay men from seminaries is like saying that the problem of juvenile delinquency is caused by children with Attention Deficit Hyperactivity Disorder.

The Vatican needs to take responsibility for, and start making genuine attempts to deal with, the real problems behind the church abuse scandal. Offender clergy need to be terminated from their positions and their identities made public. Victims of clergy abuse need to be encouraged to come forward, and their experiences should be believed and validated so that their healing can begin.

Charter on Sexual Misconduct

In June, 2002, the United States Conference of Catholic Bishops established the *Charter for the Protection of Children and Young People* for the purpose of addressing allegations of sexual abuse of minors by clergy. This document provides guidelines for all bishops as to appropriate responses to allegations of abuse. The *Charter* covers the following issues:

- Disciplining sexual offender clergy;

- Creating a safe environment for youth;

- Prompt response to allegations of abuse;

- Healing and reconciliation for victims;

- Cooperation with law enforcement and other authorities.

Although this *Charter* may perhaps be a step in the right direction in terms of acknowledging the sex abuse crisis, and gives the appearance of being based on good intentions, the document is unclear, ambiguous, and leave itself open to individual interpretation due to the lack of operational definitions. Canon law requires bishops to investigate and document reports of sexual abuse—including anonymous reports—and take appropriate action against offenders. Thomas Doyle, a canon lawyer, points out that thousands of substantiated incidents of sexual abuse by clergy have occurred over the years, and in almost all of these cases the bishops failed and/or refused to comply with canon law. The sexual abuse crimes were proven *by law enforcement officials and through lawsuits brought by the victims*—not through any efforts by the church administrators.

* * * * * * * * * * * *

I recently received a request from another SNAP member regarding possibly getting involved in a press conference in Northern California. According to the information in this person's correspondence, there is a retirement residence in the city which houses retired priests, including many previously-convicted sex offenders who are allowed to come and go as they please without any supervision or accountability whatsoever. One sex offender priest who settled a sexual abuse lawsuit for $600,000 also resides at this facility. A recent lawsuit seeking $10-million in damages alleged that the residents of this retirement home sexually molested two mentally retarded dishwashers in their employment for 30 years, while the church administration covered-up the incidents.

The retirement residence is located atop a mountain overlooking the city. The estimated value of the entire church-owned property is at least $20-million. It is a beautiful gated facility, with manicured lawns and tall palm trees, which houses approximately sixty-five priests. Upon entering the lobby, one is greeted by security personnel. I was told that security is necessary "to protect the priests." It is ironic that the *priests* seem to be in need of protection, but the church administration has taken no steps to protect the *children* of the nearby residential neighborhood against the sex offenders, or to monitor the offenders' daily activities.

SNAP members got together and spent an entire afternoon leafletting that residential area and warning parents of young children and teenagers about their neighbors at the retirement residence on the hill .

* * * * * * * * * * *

The all-important questions remain to be answered:

WHY are so many of these sexual offender priests still in the ministry?????

WHY haven't the Cardinals, Bishops, Archbishops and others who have enabled the sex offender priests been charged with crimes??????

The message they are sending to the public is, "This is a profession where you can molest a child and still keep your job."

Clergy should be held to the highest standards of appropriate conduct, and immediate action taken when they fail to uphold them. They preach about how their parishioners should refrain from engaging in immoral and illegal conduct, and people naturally expect them to practice what they preach. Words mean absolutely nothing when unsupported by conduct. Unfortunately, this inconguency between words and conduct makes a non-verbal statement to the effect that the Church and its employees cannot be trusted.

* * * * * * * * * * *

As the director for the Central Coast Counties chapter of SNAP, I advocate for victims of clergy abuse and assist with facilitation of litigation whenever necessary. The Diocese of Monterey falls within my jurisdiction.

Court records indicate that, as of this date, there have been a total of nine lawsuits filed against the Diocese of Monterey for sexual abuse by clergy. Two cases are presently before the court. Other cases were settled—one for an undisclosed amount; another for $157,000; and another for $1,500,000. In four of the cases, the Diocese was dismissed as a defendant by the court.

Notes:

NOTES:

CHAPTER FIVE:

ABUSE BY POLICE

LAW ENFORCEMENT CODE OF ETHICS

"As a law enforcement officer, my fundamental duty is to serve mankind; to safeguard lives and property; to protect the innocent against deception, the weak against oppression or intimidation, and the peaceful against violence or disorder; and to respect the Constitutional rights of all men to liberty, equality and justice.

I will keep my private life unsullied as an example to all; maintain courageous calm in the face of danger, scorn, or ridicule; develop self-restraint; and be constantly mindful of the welfare of others.

Honest in thought and deed in both my personal and official life, I will be exemplary in obeying the laws of the land and the regulations of my department. Whatever I see or hear of a confidential nature or that is confided to me in my official capacity will be kept ever secret unless revelation is necessary in the performance of my duty.

I will never act officiously or permit personal feelings, prejudices, animosities or friendships to influence my decisions. With no compromise for crime and with relentless prosecution of criminals, I will enforce the law courteously and appropriately without fear or favor, malice or ill will, never employing unnecessary force or violence and never accepting gratuities.

I recognize the badge of my office as a symbol of public faith, and I accept it as a public trust to be held as long as I am true to the ethics of the police service. I will constantly strive to achieve these objectives and ideals, dedicating myself before God to my chosen profession....law enforcement."

(Author Unknown)

* * * * * * *

A reasonable belief exists in the minds of citizens that police, in general, can be trusted. For the most part, the police make every effort to live up to the expectation that they can be trusted.

Applicants for police work have to undergo a rigorous hiring process consisting of a thorough background investigation including previous employment, education history going as far back as grammar school, criminal records, and credit records. There are the physical agility tests designed to measure an applicant's strength and dexterity, such as scaling 6-foot walls, running an obstacle course, and dragging a 150-lbs dummy a designated distance, all within a timeframe of a few minutes. Polygraph examinations and voice-stress analyses are also utilized by many police departments in screening applicants. Medical and psychological examinations are administered so as to rule-out physical and mental problems which might interfere with job efficiency. Then there's the written standardized Civil Service test. Once the applicant successfully passes this initial hiring phase, (s)he participates in additional studies at a Peace Officers Standards and Training academy. The academy curriculum includes: laws of arrest, officer safety, defense tactics, report writing, vehicle operations, weapons training, crisis intervention, jail operations, evidence collection, and various other relevant topics. For some recruits, the academy is perceived as less of an academic and professional environment and more of a "partying" situation. Indeed, when I attended the academy, the class was divided into two groups: the studiers and the partiers. Many of the partiers from out of county who had to temporarily reside in motels during the academic term took advantage of the situation in terms of cheating on their spouses and/or partners. A few were quite blatant about this behavior.

Police work is a highly stressful occupation due to its inherent dangers, particularly that of ever-increasing street violence. A police officer never knows when (s)he might be seriously injured or killed on the job. Stress is compounded by agency politics and the bureaucracy of city government; family and personal pressures; and even peer pressures.

Despite the rigorous screening and training process of applicants to police work, some having personalities unsuitable for law enforcement manage to get hired. Sometimes, these individuals are hired because they have "buddies" in police Administration who have arranged it. In recent years there has been an increase in former police officers and police chiefs coming forward and acknowledging in interviews and published autobiographies that the problem of police corruption exists to varying degrees in many law enforcement agencies.

FACTORS IN POLICE CORRUPTION

Personality Disorders

Sometimes individuals who meet the criteria for having a personality disorder are not detected in the screening process. The smooth-talking narcissist, for example, is adept at fooling people and telling them what they want to hear. The person with antisocial tendencies may be sufficiently lacking in conscience so as to be able to lie convincingly and pass polygraph tests. Others might know how to answer questions in psychological exams in such a manner as to produce mentally-stable appearing profiles.

Inadequate Stress-Coping Mechanisms

The compounding of job, family, and personal stressors along with poor coping ability can make certain officers susceptible to taking bribes, using drugs, or becoming vulnerable to the pressures of corrupt peers.

Wanting to Be A "Hero"

This is similar to the arsonist who becomes a member of the fire department and intentionally sets fires. He is usually among the first to arrive at the scene and help to extinguish the fire. This person is insecure about his/her limitations and has a need to over-compensate for them by appearing to be a "hero." One case comes to mind in which a police officer Xeroxed fingerprint cards of known criminal offenders, then "lifted" the Xeroxed prints with tape and claimed that they came from crime scenes. The police department eventually discovered the method by which this officer had been "solving" so many crimes.

Abuse of Power

The badge and gun can be deadly when worn and carried by the wrong people. Some officers have been known to use their authority for their own advantage and at the expense and victimization of others.

Addictions

Whether alcohol, sex, or drugs, addictions can render an officer extremely vulnerable to participation in other corrupt behaviors so as to maintain their habit.

Police Code of Silence

Known as the unwritten rule against "snitching" or "ratting-out" fellow officers, this "Blue Wall of Silence" only serves to obstruct justice. Police are too often expected to deliberately turn a blind eye to unethical and corrupt behaviors of other officers. Officers who become "whistle-blowers" have been subjected to retaliation, such as depicted in the movie *SERPICO* (1973).

Case Example: Sexual Abuse of Arrestee

In 1997, *Paul Martinez, a bystander at fight which occurred in a *Nevada nightclub, was arrested by several police officers. His "crime": verbal expression of concern about the responding officers' use of excessive force against another person at the scene. Martinez was beaten by the officers enroute to the police station. Upon arrival at the station, one of the arresting officers took Martinez into the restroom and sodomized him with a broom handle while another officer assisted in restraining Martinez. Both threatened to kill Martinez and his family if he reported the incident. The officers threw Martinez into a holding cell, where he began hemorrhaging violently. Inmates in the jail informed the police that Martinez needed medical assistance. Although police called for an ambulance, they informed Martinez that the situation was "not an emergency", and that the estimated time of arrival for an ambulance would be approximately "a couple of hours." At the hospital, doctors discovered that Martinez's bladder and rectum had been punctured and his injuries were determined to be of life-threatening severity. Martinez informed the hospital staff about what had occurred at the police station. A physician's assistant reported the incident to the police department's Internal Affairs unit and the news media. All of the police officers involved in this incident lied and attempted to cover-up for each other, claiming that Martinez's injuries occurred prior to his arrest during consensual sex with another man at the nightclub. It was the cops' word against his. Fortunately for Martinez, the medical and forensic evidence proved otherwise. Eventually one officer admitted to his part in the attack on Martinez, thus discrediting the others' fabrications. The officer who sodomized Martinez with the broomstick handle stuck to his story and attempted to make himself appear to be the victim in the situation. Two trials had to be conducted before three of the officers involved were found guilty of obstruction of justice. One officer was convicted of perjury.

There were many civilian and sworn employees of the police department who were present and/or witnessed the abuse but did nothing to intervene. Only seven of these people were indicted for their part in the crime.

Lack of Internal Affairs Division

Very small police departments sometimes do not have the IAD which is responsible for investigating allegations of police corruption. This can leave the door wide open for unethical and illegal conduct.

TYPES OF UNETHICAL AND CORRUPT BEHAVIORS

Fabrication of Probable Cause:

"Probable cause" is defined as circumstances which are grounds for suspicion that a law has been or is in the process of being violated, and which allow a police officer to immediately investigate the situation. Probable cause for making a traffic stop of a vehicle might include excessive speed, a brake light burned out, or weaving the vehicle across both sides of the road. Probable cause for stopping and frisking an individual might include the fact that the person is running away from a convenience store which has just been robbed, and the person matches the clothing and physical description of the robbery suspect.

Unethical and corrupt cops have been known to fabricate the existence of probable cause so as to justify their conduct. For example, years ago, a State Trooper who made traffic stops of vehicles driven by attractive women, claiming that their "rear lights weren't working" or their "tires appeared to be low on air," was eventually arrested and convicted for the rape and murder of many of these women. In another situation, an officer ordered a suspect not to move. Although the suspect complied, the officer shot the suspect and attempted to justify the use of excessive and unreasonable force with fabricated probable cause. Fortunately for the victim, the entire event was caught on video-tape by security cameras.

Preferential Treatment for Gratuities:

Many citizens like to acknowledge the hard work of police officers by giving them occasional gifts or doing favors for them. For example, a restaurant owner might provide free coffee to officers who stop by during their break times. While gratuities which are offered in good-faith to indicate appreciation might be appropriate, it is those that are given—and expected—in exchange for preferential treatment that create major problems.

Accessories to Crime

Corrupt officers have been known to deliberately "look the other way" regarding criminal activity by people who have bribed them with money, gifts, or favors, and who have made it clear that they expect selective enforcement from the officers.

Refusal to Back-Up Non-Corrupt Officers:

This presents an officer safety issue in that, when officers refuse to assist fellow officers, or when they deliberately respond slower to back-up requests, lives may become endangered. Modern police vehicle tracking technology can help to prevent this.

Planting False Evidence:

Corrupt officers are notorious for making arrests based on false evidence which they have planted at an alleged crime scene, for the purpose of setting-up certain people to be arrested and/ or charged with the commission of a crime. For example, while searching the residence of a parolee whom the police and/or community do not want residing in a certain neighborhood, officers might "find" drugs, a weapon, or other contraband, so as to score points with the community for sending the parolee back to prison.

In California, a Los Angeles police officer was recently charged with making false arrests via planting false evidence. This same officer had two civil lawsuits filed against him for similar conduct, which the city settled for $520,000.

Procurement of false evidence might also include the coercion of false confessions by innocent persons, as to commission of crimes, via abuse of the polygraph, bullying, threats, and other unethical interrogation tactics.

Not Submitting All Evidence Collected:

This occurs most commonly in drug busts whereby officers who confiscate, for example, 50 lbs of marijuana and $500,000 will submit only half of the amounts into evidence and use and/or sell the portion which they have retained.

Similarly, theft of evidence, extortion of money and/or property, and theft of police department supplies and equipment occurs on a regular basis. In 2004, the Los Angeles County Sheriff's Department's Office of Independent Review reported their findings which included: sexual abuse, drug dealing, driving while intoxicated, using excessive force, theft and extortion, and sales of police equipment on eBay. They also found 800 uninvestigated claims of police misconduct.

Falsifying Case Reports:

It is common practice for corrupt officers to embellish and/ or altogether falsify case reports—often referred to as "creative report-writing"—so as to make crime victims look bad, cover-up their own illegal or unethical conduct, and make certain criminal suspects appear worse than they actually are. It is also not unheard of for case reports not to be taken at all; to become "lost in the shuffle" of paperwork; or to be completely fabricated by corrupt officers.

Additionally, law enforcement agencies have been known to attempt to cover-up for their officers with regard to complaints filed by citizens simply by shredding complaint reports, thus rendering investigation and prosecution impossible.

Sexual Abuse and Harassment:

Sexual abuse and harassment—of fellow officers, citizens, police cadets, and crime suspects—is not a rare occurrence in the law enforcement field. Female officers and gay officers have been targets of harassment for years. Many years ago, female police officers were sparse, as police work was considered to be "for boys only." It is now very common to see increasing numbers of women stepping out of patrol cars and sitting in police academy classrooms. Women used to be subjected to sexual harassment in the police academies and on the job. Complaints by these women were perceived by their instructors and supervisors as "weaknesses" and "over-sensitivity." Many female victims of sexual harassment were constructively discharged, this being justified by supervisors and academy instructors by stating that, "If they can't handle it (the harassment) here in a controlled environment, then they can't handle it out on the street." The situation was even worse for the gay officer in cities which were anti-gay. Fortunately, times have changed. Anti-discrimination laws have played a major part in paving the road for women and gays interested in law enforcement as a career.

Case Example: Mishandling of Sexual Misconduct Complaint

In 2002, *Stephanie, a female detective of the department *Illinois police department made a complaint about a male veteran detective of the department who had forced her to perform oral sex on him more than a decade prior in exchange for protection of her teenaged son who had been a police informant. Stephanie did not report the incident at the time of its occurrence because she was afraid that the male detective would retaliate by killing her son or arranging to have him killed.

The Internal Affairs office conducted a very cursory eighteen-month investigation of Stephanie's sexual harassment complaint. They failed to contact witnesses or follow-up on leads. The detective in question was allowed to remain on active duty, even though typically, during an investigation, an officer is placed on administrative leave. The head of the Internal Affairs office informed Stephanie that her case was "inconclusive" and therefore would be closed. Ironically, the determination had been based on nothing but the detective's denial of the allegations. Stephanie filed an appeal, and six months later was informed that the original determination of the case as inconclusive was correct. The police department's apparent priority was to protect one of its "good old boys."

A citizen review panel later recommended that the police chief once again review the investigation of her complaint.

Case Example: Sexual Harassment of Transsexual

*Tony Weston was a middle-aged female-to-male transsexual, formerly *Toni Weston, who was accused of physically assaulting another person at a support group for transsexuals in *Nevada. The alleged victim made a complaint to the police, but the district attorney's office declined to file formal charges against Tony.

Approximately a year later, a detective from the juvenile division of the local police department called Tony and claimed to have a warrant for his arrest. The detective offered to cancel the warrant in exchange for a sexual massage. The detective arranged a meeting at Tony's residence. Upon arrival at Tony's residence the detective bragged about having "clout" within the police department and court system. He also convinced Tony that it would be a waste of time to discuss the matter of the outstanding warrant with police administration or the court staff.

The following week the detective again met with Tony at Tony's home. At some point in the conversation, the detective propositioned him. Unbeknownst to the detective, Tony caught the entire incident on tape by means of a video camera which he had cleverly hidden in his living room. Several weeks later, Tony consulted with an attorney who was also the director of a legal advocacy organization for the gay, lesbian, and trans-gendered community. The attorney advised him to file a complaint with the police department's Internal Affairs office. Upon reviewing the complaint, investigators from the Internal Affairs office arranged to meet at Tony's home for the purposes of wiretapping a call to the detective. The detective again called Tony to arrange for another sexual massage session, and the conversation was caught on tape.

A month later, the police chief informed Tony informed by letter that the findings of the investigation showed only that the detective was in violation of department policy, not that he had committed a crime. The letter also stated that the case would be handled on an administrative level versus as a criminal matter. The detective's sanction consisted of a non-paid 32-day suspension.

This department's policy stated that police officers under investigation are eligible to have their personnel files purged after six years if they are not charged with a crime, and are not caught repeating the conduct in question. Approximately six years subsequent to this incident, the detective continued to be employed with the same police department.

PEACE OFFICERS BILL OF RIGHTS

In 1977, California became the first state to enact a Bill of Rights for peace officers, which was signed into law by Governor Jerry Brown, and supported by the ACLU. The text of the POBR can be found in *California Government Code § 3300-3312.*

The POBR legally allows police departments to keep citizen complaints against police officers, and any disciplinary records of officers, secret. This is applicable even to officers with histories of repeated misconduct. Questions have arisen with regard to whether the secrecy is necessary and/or violates the rights of citizens, in consideration of the fact that police are public servants who should be held accountable to the public which is, in effect, their employer. Police argue that their reputations need to be protected, and that allowing citizens access to police disciplinary records would leave officers vulnerable to public mistrust. The issue remains open to debate.

* * * * * * * * * * * * * * * * * * *

As for citizen ride-alongs, whereby a citizen may "ride-along" with a patrol officer in order to experience what a typical shift is like for a law enforcement officer, certain male officers have been known to attempt to sexualize the encounter. Although this may be consensual activity between two adults, an issue exists as to whether the citizen felt pressured or compelled to "comply" with the requests of the officer simply because of his position, and whether the citizen was deprived of his or her rights under color of law while being complicit. In 2004 a Los Angeles County deputy sheriff who had used his position of authority to force women to have sex with him was indicted on civil rights violations. As the result of an investigation conducted by the Federal Bureau of Investigation and the

Los Angeles County Sheriff's Department, he was charged with four felony counts and one misdemeanor count. A jury found the deputy guilty of all charges in 2006.

Prostitutes—aka "sex workers"—have been vulnerable to sexual abuse and harassment by police because of their profession. After all, how likely is it that a person with a history of prostitution arrests—probably a drug addict—reporting rape or sexual abuse by a cop, is going to be taken seriously?

Police explorer cadets, typically students under the legal age of consent, have also been victims of sexual abuse by police officers who have a sexual attraction to teenagers and the power to determine the cadet's future in law enforcement

Enabling Other Corrupt Cops/Professionals:

This category would include any kind of action, or failure to act, on the part of fellow officers which conceals and/or enables the behavior of corrupt officers or professionals.

Case Example: Police Intimidation of Sexual Abuse Victims

In 1992, approximately half a dozen African-American boys in Chicago were sexually molested on multiple occasions by Father Vincent Stewart (now deceased). When the boys attempted to report the abuse to the police, they were later picked up by plain-clothes detectives from the police department who ordered them to remain silent about the incidents. The detectives made threats to the boys' safety and that of their families. It was suspected that one of Father Stewart's relatives who was on the police force at the time instigated the detention of and threats to the teenaged boys. The case against Stewart and the church was eventually settled for three-million dollars.

Case Example: Supervising Officer Enabling Sexual Predator Reserve Officer

*Bob Potter was a member of several City government committees, worked as a reserve police officer for the *New York police department, and served on several social organizations throughout the county.

Potter is described as an individual who meets the criteria for Narcissistic Personality Disorder. Additionally, he was a pathological liar and a sexual predator of teenaged girls, with a general reputation for being a "womanizer", flirting with and attempting to seduce everyone in a skirt, despite the fact that he was married and had a family. His status in the community served to disillusion the community into believing that he was a totally respectable and law-abiding citizen. The husband of a woman with whom he reportedly had an ongoing affair was alleged to have told his wife that he felt sorry for the mistress(es)/girlfriend(s) with whom Potter was involved, because in the end Potter would see that the woman(en) got the shaft while Potter himself came out smelling like a rose.

During an investigative assignment Potter met an attractive teenager named *Susan, who was a friend of one of the witnesses in the case. Susan described how Potter would flirt with her------constantly telling her that she was beautiful and that he thought about her all the time. Potter apparently sensed that Susan was from a dysfunctional family, had low self-esteem, and was vulnerable. She would meet him at the police department parking lot on weekends and evenings, and accompany him on ride-alongs. After several months of grooming Susan with compliments and promises, Potter finally persuaded her to have sex with him. The relationship became short-lived when Susan was informed by one of the police cadets that Potter had had sex with another police officer's ex-girlfriend the previous weekend. When Susan confronted Potter, he simply denied it. However, reliable witnesses confirmed to Susan that the incident actually occurred.

Potter eventually met another teenaged girl, *Rachel, at a high school football game at which she was a cheerleader. After the game, he took Rachel aside and flirted with her, telling her that she was beautiful, and that he would "gladly trade places" with her boyfriend anytime. As it turned out, Rachel did not have a boyfriend. Potter invited her to meet him for a soda at a designated café. He took her on many ride-alongs in his patrol car, over the next dew months, each time flirting with her and touching her affectionately in non-sexual ways, and bragging about the alleged power that he had in the community.

Potter eventually persuaded Rachel to have sex with him, telling her that he was awaiting a divorce from his wife, whom he portrayed as a cold bitch who had supposedly withheld sex from him for years. He also told her that since he was affiliated with the police department he had "bodyguards" who were constantly looking out for him and who wouldn't hesitate to kill anybody— or their friends and family—who caused him any trouble. This was supposed to be a "subtle" warning to Rachel not to tell anybody about their relationship, since she was a minor. He reassured Rachel that he was "basically a nice guy" but if she were to ever get angry at him and try to report him for statutory rape he would see to it that Rachel could never be able to call the police for help, again, in her life. That is, if she wasn't killed, first, or put in prison for a crime which she did not commit, based on "circumstantial evidence." Potter claimed to have been involved in cases whereby innocent people were arrested and incarcerated in Mexican jails where they did not have any rights and where no justice existed. Rachel initially didn't believe Potter' story about how the police wouldn't ever help her, again, if she reported him—after all, it was the police department's job to protect and to serve—until one day when Potter introduced her to his supervisor on the police force, *Lieutenant Cooper. Cooper apparently was a close friend of Potter and had arranged for Potter to be hired as a reserve police officer. He was fully aware of Potter' sexual pursuits of women and teenaged girls. Cooper make a comment to Potter, in front of Rachel, to the effect of "putting a contract out on" somebody, so that Cooper and Potter, "won't have to worry about him, any-more." That comment, made by the police Lieutenant, convinced Rachel that she had every reason to fear for her life if she were to tell anyone about her relationship with Potter.

This relationship was ongoing for approximately four years, until Rachel became of legal age, and Potter became increasingly abusive toward her, making it clear that she "wasn't as exciting" to him since she wasn't a minor, anymore. On one occasion, while his wife was away for a couple of weeks, Potter invited Rachel to a men-only poker party at his house. Entertainment at the party consisted of pornographic movies from the police evidence locker, provided by Cooper and Potter. After considerable drinking had occurred, Potter coerced Rachel into having sex with each of the men at the party—including Lieutenant Cooper. Rachel later discovered that Potter was paid in advance by the men for her sexual services. She was nineteen years old at the time she was subjected to this treatment.

When Rachel terminated this relationship and attempted to report Potter to the police, Cooper created interference by not only refusing to take a report on Potter, but by falsifying reports about Rachel. Additionally, Cooper and Potter intimidated Rachel, via threats to her life, into making a false confession as to "harassing" Potter at his home. This false confession was subsequently written into a police report by Cooper.

Potter would continue to intimidate Rachel by driving past her apartment and/or place of employment, glaring at her if they saw each other. When Potter was on police duty and saw Rachel riding in a vehicle with another man, he would pull the man's vehicle over as though conducting a routine traffic stop, and tell the man that Rachel was a prostitute and that he could be arrested for soliciting. Potter also spread rumors around town that he had to "buy Rachel off with a large sum of money" so that she would not tell his wife about their affair.

Rachel became so distraught over these situations that she moved to another state so as to get away from Potter and his crowd. Despite physically relocating, Rachel experienced symptoms consistent with Post-Traumatic Stress Disorder and Rape Trauma Syndrome for years. She stopped wearing feminine clothes and makeup, cut her long hair extremely short, and became morbidly obese so as not to be attractive to men.

Cooper reportedly managed to work his way all the way up to the position of Chief of Police in the same police department. Potter simply continued his behavior with new teenaged victims.

* * * * * * * * * * * * * * * *

COMMUNICATING THE WRONG MESSAGE TO CIZITENS

Law enforcement officers are supposed to provide protection for citizens regardless of race, socio-economic status, gender, sexual orientation, disability, age, and national origin.

Police, whether by committing abuse or enabling it, communicate the wrong messages to the public. Specifically, this behavior tells the public that they might as well remain complacent because nothing will be done about sexual abuse and police corruption—at least, not by the police department.

It classifies police officers into categories of "good cops" and "bad cops" and citizens are at a disadvantage in terms of being unable to identify which cops are in either category. This makes the "good cops" look bad and ultimately communicates the message that "cops can't be trusted."

Corrupt police officers need to be held accountable for their crimes and terminated from the law enforcement profession. Citizens should not have to worry about the possibility of being abused by the officers who have been hired to protect them.

Notes:

Notes:

PART TWO:

THE VICTIMS

CHAPTER SIX:

THE VICTIM'S EXPERIENCE

IMPACT AND EFFECTS ON VICTIMS

This section will focus on "complicit" sexual relationships occurring between adult professionals and persons under the legal age of consent, as opposed to cases involving forcible rape. However, this is not to state or imply that rape victims do not experience similar emotional and/or psychological damage. Numerous psychology and self-help books have been written on the subject of recovering from the effects of sexual assault. This section will simply describe a few of the numerous effects which can have a lasting impact on the victims. A thorough description of the entire range of the psychological and emotional ramifications experienced by sexual abuse victims is beyond the scope and purpose of this book.

* * * * * * * *

A distinction needs to be made with regard to the terms "impact" and "effect." Impact suggests a "collision," of sorts, resulting from a degree of force that has been exerted. It also might refer to being "stuck" in an abnormal position, such as impacted wisdom teeth. A colleague of mine refers to the impact of sexual abuse as similar to being hit by a Mack truck. The force in question can be mental or physical, or a combination of both, and can leave the person impacted, or "stuck," in a position whereby (s)he is unable to grow and develop normally. Effect implies a change associated with an impacting event. Effects tend to be behavioral, mental, emotional, and physical, and may be attempts to adapt to an impact. With regard to the Mack truck analogy, the situation is identical to that of a felony hit-and-run case, with the perpetrator as the driver. In cases of child sexual abuse, the physical impact is

the actual abuse. The emotional impact is one of progressively killing the victim by taking away his or her capacity to be a normal
child, adolescent, or adult. The victim is forced to live with the
effects of the abuse for the rest of his or her life. When a child is
sexually abused by a trusted professional, (s)he is impacted in such
a manner as to result in various devastating effects. Normal issues
which are consistent with childhood and adolescence will become
extremely and painfully confounded.

Children and adolescents are vulnerable human beings simply because of their status as children or adolescents. Very young
children have limited skills with regard to speech, comprehen-
sion, and self-expression, and are usually taught to obey adults un-
questioningly. Their small size renders them unable to physically
defend themselves against large, aggressive, and violent adults.
Adolescents, despite possibly having some capability of physical
resistance, are often verbally coerced by threats, guilt, and promises, into complying with the abuser.

PSYCHOLOGICAL EFFECTS

Some of the effects of sexual abuse on a victim include but are
not limited to the following:

False Sense of Intimacy

When a victim is seduced by a trusted professional (s)he may
believe that their "relationship" is "special." Typically, the perpetrator will have made statements to this effect. It is not uncommon for victims to confuse sex and love, or to equate the two.
Sometimes, victims will feel "special" because the perpetrator selected him or her over others. This is reinforced by positive and/or
affectionate statements from the perpetrator, such as, "I love you"
or, "You really make my day!" Young victims who do not experi-

ence genuine affection within their family tend to be the most vulnerable to smooth-talking sexual predators, since the predator appears to be filling an emotional need of the victim which isn't being met by the victim's parents.

Confusion

Victims often wonder, "Why me?" Sometimes victims will attempt to answer that question by correlating the seduction and abuse with some other behavioral or intra-personal trait. For example, a teenaged victim who is an academic underachiever might assume that the perpetrator is not sexually involved with students who earn good grades and therefore it was the bad grades that "caused" the perpetrator to become attracted to the victim.

Inability to Trust as Adults

In many cases, the effects of child sexual abuse do not manifest for as long as decades. In these cases, victims often find themselves unable to trust others or establish intimate relationships. They may be dislike being touched, and may develop psychosomatic illnesses.

Shame

Shame is a state whereby the victim feels there is something wrong with him or her as a person. Shame differs from guilt in that guilt is usually associated with one's conduct as opposed to one's inner self. Abuse victims tend to experience chronic shame because they believe that, on some level, there is something bad about him or her that caused the abuse to happen.

Anxiety and Hyper-vigilance

Anxiety may pertain to having to keep the abuse secret. Children under the age of consent risk discovery of the abuse and subsequent "punishment" for the perpetrator's crimes, such as being sent to foster or group home placement. In these situations, the victim is usually separated from siblings and pets, and established friendships become disrupted if the placement site is in another county or state.

Hyper-vigilance may result from believing the perpetrator's stories about how his "buddies" are constantly spying on the victim or threats to inflict harm to and/or kill the victim.

Post-Traumatic Stress Disorder

While experiencing PTSD, survivors of abuse may behave as though the abusive events are happening in the present. Any seemingly insignificant thing might be a potential trigger of PTSD symptoms, which can include depression, anxiety, obsessions, nightmares, insomnia, panic attacks, and "body-memories" whereby the abuse is re-experienced via physiological sensations.

Feeling Worthless

This is a belief that one has very little or no value. Considering that a sexual abuse victim's boundaries are violated, the perpetrator has no respect for the victim, and perhaps other adults have not been supportive toward the victim, it is not difficult to understand why victims would feel worthless. The message here is, "You don't matter."

Depression

This typically begins with feelings of powerlessness and helplessness. The victim believes that (s)he cannot change his or her situation: the perpetrator will not change; the sense of shame and guilt will not go away; and perhaps others who should be supportive and helpful to the victim just aren't doing their job.

Feeling that one has no control over one's situation eventually can lead to a state of learned helplessness and severe depression. People often ask, "Why didn't the victim just leave (the relationship)?" and, "Why didn't the victim just stop seeing the abuser and turn him in to the police?" While these may sound like easy solutions to the problem, unfortunately they can be very difficult if not impossible for the victim to implement. Studies on learned helplessness have been conducted using dogs as experimental subjects, whereby the dogs were confined to a small space and given electric shocks whenever they attempted to escape. Eventually the dogs realized that regardless of what they did they were going to get electrocuted, so they gave up trying to escape. Sexual abuse victims who cannot terminate the relationship with the abuser and are responsible for other people's lives by maintaining silence about the abuse are in a similar situation as those dogs. One victim who was repeatedly abused by several male school staff attempted to report the abuse to the school principal. The victim was told that he had better "keep quiet" because if he didn't they would fire his father, who was employed as a custodian at the same school. The victim learned to suffer in silence. Depression can occur gradually or suddenly. The victim loses interest in his or her usual activities, and very little seems to matter, anymore. Expending energy for what does matter seems draining and overwhelming. Left untreated, depression can progress and ultimately lead to suicide.

Compulsion for Re-Victimization

This refers to a sexual abuse victim's unconscious "attraction" to people who may become abusive in some manner, including sexually. This is common in battered women who unconsciously become attracted to violent men, just because violence is all that they feel they can relate to.

TERRI AUSTIN, PH.D., J.D.

NOTES:

NOTES:

CHAPTER SEVEN:

SURVIVAL STRATEGIES

Stockholm Syndrome

Stockholm Syndrome is considered to be the ultimate survival strategy for victims of abuse. The term originated from an incident in Stockholm, Sweden in 1973 consisting of a six-day hostage situation during what is known as the Norrmalmstorg Robbery. The hostages, three women and a man, were confined to the bank's vault. The captors strapped dynamite to them and snare traps were set up so that, in the event of any rescue attempts by police whatsoever, the hostages would be killed.   Throughout the six-day ordeal, the hostages psychologically bonded with their captors to the point of becoming friends with them and manifesting resistance to being rescued. When the captors were arrested, the hostages set up a fund to assist with legal fees and supported them through the court process. Later, one of the hostages married one of the captors.

This is a type of paradoxical, unconscious psychological and emotional bonding which can occur between victims and abusers in situations wherein there is an imbalance of power. The victim who perceives that (s)he cannot escape from his or her situation minimizes the dangerousness of the situation. (S)he focuses on the "positive" qualities and small kindnesses of the abuser to the point of believing that the abuser loves him or her, and will protect the abuser from criminal prosecution. Victims who develop Stockholm Syndrome have an extremely difficult time psychologically separating from the abuser. It is not uncommon for them to continue to protect the abuser for many years despite physical separation.

Sexual abuse victims, like hostages, prisoners of war, and cult members, learn to develop cognitive and behavioral survival strategies in attempts to minimize pain and tolerate their abuse situation, over which they perceive they have no control or

means of escape. Hostages have been known to utilize medita-
tion, imagery, nurturing, and prayer so as to maintain a sense of
optimism and hope. The following are some survival strategies
used by victims of interpersonal violence.

Silence

Victims of sexual abuse who are in complicit "relationships"
with perpetrators are given a disproportionate degree of responsibility for other people's lives via maintaining silence and secrecy
about the abuse. The victim's silence enables the perpetrator to stay
out of jail and keep his job. The perpetrator basically gets to have
his cake and eat it, too. If the perpetrator is married, the victim's
silence assures that the perpetrator's wife and children do not find
out about his extra-marital "affair." Already-present problems in
the perpetrator's marriage can continue to be avoided. The victim's
silence also "keeps the peace" in his or her own family, especially
if the perpetrator has been a longtime friend of the family. The
victim is forced to give the outward impression that "everything
is OK" despite the fact that it is not. (S)he learns to suppress feelings; to hide things such as drugs or gifts from the perpetrator,
and to lie to parents and friends about his or her actual where-
abouts and activities, so as not to get caught. (S)he learns to make
up excuses and alibis in the event that anything is suspected and
(s)he is questioned by anyone. This magnitude of responsibility for
other people's lives is one which nobody—especially children or
adolescents—should have to shoulder

Denial

Many victims live in a state of subconscious denial of the
harmful effects of their situation and will not acknowledge the
perpetrator's conduct as abuse until many years later. This is particularly true of child and adolescent victims whose parents are

emotionally abusive or neglectful and for whom the perpetrator fills an emotional void. It is similar to drug users, alcoholics and smokers who deny the consequences of the vices----they think it isn't hurting them but, in actuality, it is.

Boiling Frog Syndrome

Relative to denial is a behavioral pattern referred to as the "Boiling Frog Syndrome." This is based on the fact that if a frog is thrown into a container of boiling water, it will jump out, as would be expected. However, if the frog is placed in the container of water and the temperature of the water gradually increased to the boiling point, the frog will stay in the container until it dies, simply because it has acclimated itself to the gradually changing temperature which it perceives all along to be normal. Sexual abuse victims are in a similar situation in that their tolerance to the abuse increases over time and they may perceive the conduct as normal without realizing that damage is actually being done.

Dissociation

Another survival strategy is that of dissociation, whereby a victim will simply "zone-out" during the abuse. It is a state of being physically present while at the same time psychologically absent so as not to fully experience something which is happening. We all have done this to an extent, for instance, during dental procedures. Students dissociate in class so as to detach themselves from boring lectures. Dissociation may be a means of temporarily compensating for a lack of control over an unpleasant situation.

Dissociation can also manifest as a psychological disorder. The *DSM-IV* (A.P.A., 1994) lists the following types of dissociative disorders:

- *Dissociative Amnesia:* : an inability to recall important personal information, usually of a traumatic or stressful nature, that is too extensive to be explained by ordinary forgetfulness;

- *Dissociative Fugue:* sudden, unexpected travel away from home or one's customary place of work, accompanied y an inability to recall one's past and confusion about personal identity or the assumption of a new identity;

- *Dissociative Identity Disorder:* the presence of two or more distinct identities or personality states that recurrently take control of the individual's behavior accompanied by an inability to recall important personal information that is too extensive to be explained by ordinary forgetfulness;

- *Depersonalization Disorder:* a persistent or recurrent felling of being detached from one's mental process or body that is accompanied by intact reality testing;

- *Dissociation Disorder Not Otherwise Specified:* is included for disorders in which the predominant feature is a dissociative symptom, but that do not meet the criteria for any of the above-specified Dissociative Disorders.

[Copyright 2000 by the American Psychiatric Association, Washington, D.C. Use of this material is by permission of the publisher. www.apa.org .]

* * * * * *

With regard to survival strategies in general, human beings have two basic responses to dangerous or threatening situations: fight or flight. When neither is possible, the ultimate result is the loss of self.

NOTES:

Terri Austin, Ph.D., J.D.

NOTES:

CHAPTER EIGHT:

THE PERPETRATOR'S DEFENSES

Sex offenders have an entire arsenal of defenses, excuses, and justifications for their conduct if and when they are discovered or confronted, accused of committing a sex crime, arrested, or named as defendants in civil litigation proceedings. These range from simple denial to the "Twinkie Defense." Many perpetrators have planned their defenses far in-advance and will resort to extreme measures to make the victim appear to be the "bad guy." Perpetrators have even denied knowing the victim, despite having known the victim for many years.

Denial

First and foremost of these defenses is outright denial. Sex offenders will deny, deny, and deny—and then deny some more! In one situation, a police officer caught a priest *with his pants down* in a car with a fourteen-year-old boy—and the priest denied that anything sexual was occurring.

An issue worthy of mention is that of wives or partners of sexual perpetrators who "stand by their men." These individuals are either in a state of total denial—or are conscious accessories to their partner's crime. This may be similar to the dynamics in incestuous families where the non-abusing parent doesn't see what is happening when it is occurring right under their nose—sometimes even in the adjoining room. Reasons for the spouse or partner remaining in denial, despite having a sense that "something" isn't quite right, include low self-esteem, a belief that (s)he cannot survive without the husband or partner, fear of him, the belief that he will eventually change, and not wanting to ruin his reputation by leaving him.

Case Example: Denial by Priest's Wife and Parishioners

*Father Bill Farrington, a *Washington Espiscopal priest,

was accused of and admitted to having sex with a female minor for four years beginning when the victim was thirteen years old. Father Farrington, removed from his ministry in the early summer of 2006, attempted to justify his conduct on the grounds that it was a "consensual relationship." When SNAP members leafleted in front of Farrington's church just before mass, Farrington's wife ran out of the church and demanded that SNAP members surrender all of the flyers. When they refused, she attempted to grab flyers out of one SNAP member's hand. The woman stated that the sexual abuse incident was "water under the bridge," because it happened a long time ago and her husband had apologized for his conduct.

One of the members of the congregation, a rather large man, threatened to "knock [a SNAP member] on [his] ass" if the leafleting did not stop. Another individual, a woman, stated that she would not hesitate to leave her teenaged daughters alone with Father Farrington----she had that much trust in him. A SNAP member told this woman that she needed to tell a psychotherapist about the fact that she would not hesitate to leave her teenaged daughters alone with an admitted child molester.

After the church service concluded, members of the congregation driving out of the parking lot yelled profanities at SNAP members. A lady estimated to be in her seventies glared at a SNAP member and flipped him the middle finger. SNAP members recall being referred to as "asshole" at least a couple of dozen times.

* * * * * * * *

Consent

Many sex offenders will allege that the sexual activity was consensual, or that the victim was the one who initiated it. It is all supposedly the victim's fault—never mind the fact that the perpetrator, a professional adult, has the responsibility to act like an adult and behave appropriately. Sex offenders will insist that they tried to discontinue the sexual activity—but the victim black-mailed them into continuing it. In one case involving a Catholic diocese in Kentucky, church officials named as defendants in a child abuse lawsuit stated that the thirteen-year-old victim was comparatively negligent. In other words, according to the church, the victim was partly responsible for the sexual abuse which he experienced because he allegedly consented to the defendants' conduct. Remember, persons under the legal age of consent cannot give consent; and in situations where a power imbalance exists, they cannot give *informed* consent. The situation is an emotional form of extortion, similar to one in which a child complicitly surrenders his or her lunch money to the bigger, tougher kid who demands that (s)he do so.

Blaming the Victim

Relative to denial are allegations by the perpetrator that the victim is lying. The perpetrator will zero-in on some aspect of the victim's vulnerability and blow it all out of proportion so as to diminish the victim's credibility. This is not difficult to do, considering that most sexual perpetrators who have been acquainted with the victim for a period of time prior to the abuse often know the victim better than the victim's own parents do. The perpetrator who is also a mental health professional has the advantage of knowing the victim on a psycho-dynamic level, and will use this information as a manipulation tool. Common attempts to diminish the victim's credibility include: the victim is promiscuous; the victim started the whole thing; the victim is a drug user—(s)he is having drug-induced delusions and/or hallucinations; the victim has behavior problems and a criminal record—why believe a juvenile delinquent?; and the victim is fabricating the incident. While there have been cases in which individuals have made false allegations of child abuse, these tend not to happen very frequently.

"Victim is the Bad Guy": Falsification of Evidence

Often, sexual abuse victims are accused by sex offenders as being "crazy" or "psychotic", and "hallucinating" or "imagining" the sexual abuse incidents. In one case, the perpetrator's attorney accused the victim of being a "highly mentally disturbed young man who fabricated a story about his therapist."

Sexual perpetrators will falsify evidence so as to make the victim appear to be stalking them. This is done by alleging that the victim's normal, non-criminal behaviors—e.g., sending cards, giving gifts, visiting, maintaining contact through phone calls or letters—have been done with the intent to stalk and harass the perpetrator. The perpetrator tries to give the impression that he was just minding his own business when along came this child, teenager, or young adult who, for no reason, decided to disrupt the perpetrator's life with unwanted, unsolicited, stalking behaviors. In one case, a counselor made up *in-advance* a fictitious "list" of phone calls which the victim allegedly made to his residence, and a list of "letters" allegedly sent by the victim, during a time period in which he was sexually abusing the victim. At no time did he ever tell the victim not to contact him. At one point, when he suspected that the victim would report him to the police, the perpetrator contacted the police and made a false report about being "stalked" by the victim. When the victim, a young adult male whom the perpetrator had abused since the victim was a teenager, finally reported the sexual abuse to the police, police refused to believe him because of all of the "evidence" which the perpetrator had accumulated. The victim was threatened with a restraining order by law enforcement officers who did not want to be bothered with investigating all of the facts of the case, as it appeared that the victim had emotional problems. In another case, the perpetrator typed letters to himself and forced his teenaged victim to sign them. He then showed them to other people, claiming the letters were "evidence" that the victim was attempting to seduce him.

Case Example: Cameron Hooker, Sexual Enslavement of Young Adult

In 1977, a young twenty-year-old female adult was abducted while hitchhiking and held captive as a sex slave for seven years in California. Her captor, Cameron Hooker, convinced her that he belonged to a secret society of sex slave owners, and that the members of this society looked out for each other. He informed her that the Society would kill her and harm her family if she attempted to escape. The victim believed that she had no means of escape. She was subjected to torture, rape, and forced to participate in sexual acts in which she normally would not have participated. At times, she was confined for days to a coffin-like box underneath Hooker's bed. Hooker typed love letters to himself, forced the victim to sign them, and kept these documents to use as "evidence" that the victim was a consenting and willing participant in the event that his crimes should ever be discovered. Hooker eventually was arrested after the victim escaped subsequent to Hooker's wife disclosing that her husband fabricated the story about belonging to a sex slave society. Hooker was convicted of his crimes in or about 1987, and is presently serving a prison sentence.

* * * * * * * * * *

Destruction of Evidence: "Victim Can't Prove It"

Destruction of evidence parallels the falsification of evidence. Although any sexual perpetrator would not hesitate to destroy evidence of his guilt and/or falsify evidence of his innocence in order to avoid prison, this might occur more frequently amongst police officers who happen to be sexual predators simply because they have the most control over what goes into the evidence lockers and crime reports. They have more power than the average perpetrator to interfere with the investigation process and obstruct justice. As an example, a victim submitted pornographic photographs to the police which were taken of him as a teenager by another officer who was a crime scene photographer. The photographs somehow got "lost," at the police station and the victim was alleged to have made a false report. In another case, a perpetrator falsified evidence by having his friends make obscene phone calls to his secretary from the sexual abuse victim's home, unbeknownst to the victim. The perpetrator's intent was to set the victim up, knowing that tracing equipment had been installed on his office line and the calls would be traced to the victim's phone. Since the perpetrator was at his office during the time that the obscene phone calls came in, it was impossible for the victim to prove the perpetrator's involvement. Police warned the victim that he could be arrested for "harassing" the perpetrator.

Victim Was Not Damaged

Another defense tactic is to allege that the conduct did not constitute abuse, and/or that the victim was not harmed by it. One SNAP survivor described the various legal tactics which were utilized by the defendant's attorneys in attempts to coerce her into dropping her case against several Catholic priests. Initially, they denied that sexual abuse occurred. Then, they claimed that the victim was not harmed because, "...priests masturbating in front of children does not constitute sexual abuse..."

"Victim Cannot Forgive"

This is a favorite attempt at diversion by sex offenders in the clergy. Victims are expected to "be good Christians and forgive and forget." It is implied that the victim's refusal or inability to forgive the perpetrator makes him or her a sinner. (S)he is the "bad guy" if (s)he doesn't forgive the perpetrator. All of the damage inflicted by the perpetrator is expected to be minimized by a simple apology from the perpetrator, which the victim is expected to accept unconditionally "as Christ would have done."

The term "forgive" can have different meanings. It can mean letting go of hatred and resentment. Or it can be equated with "pardon," which is unconditionally granted and excuses the offender without penalty. "Forgiveness," however the victim may choose to operationally define it, is not a requirement for healing from the effects of sexual abuse. In light of the fact that "consent" cannot be given without a complete understanding of all of the potential risks involved in a situation, likewise, "forgiveness" cannot happen without a complete understanding on the part of the victim of the extent of the damages likely to result from a situation.

Forgiving a perpetrator has the potential to set the victim up for further victimization. Perpetrators' apologies are rarely sincere. They are only "sorry" that they got caught! Sex offenders—especially preferential child molesters—will not change their behavior just because it has hurt or offended another person.

The decision to forgive or not should be ultimately that of the victim. Forgiveness should not be coerced by the imposition of guilt or shame tactics by the offender and/or the offender's supporting institution

"Twinkie Defenses"

Sexual abuse perpetrators have gone so far as to admit to the commission of the crime while attempting to deflect responsibility with various justifications. Some of these include, "I was drunk at the time I did it"; "I didn't know what I was doing, at the time;" "Temporary insanity;" "I had a terrible childhood;" "I thought (s) he was an adult;" and, "The devil made me do it."

Sure. And their dogs more than likely ate their homework...

Notes:

NOTES:

PART THREE:

INTERVENTION

CHAPTER NINE:

"RED FLAGS"

This chapter will address some warning signs—"red flags"—that sexual abuse might be occurring, and situations which might inadvertently predispose children or adolescents to abuse. While many of the issues addressed have been correlated with sexual abuse, it is important to remember that the presence of any or all of these issues does not necessarily mean that abuse is in fact happening. The only way to determine whether or not a child or adolescent is being abused is by thorough investigation. Certain types of family dynamics, suspicious conduct from professionals, and behaviors on the part of the victim, should be red flags to people who are in mandated reporter occupations as well as the law enforcement field.

* * * * * * * * * *

FAMILY DYNAMICS

Emotionally Unavailable Parents

Victims of sexual abuse maintain silence for a number of reasons, some of which have been previously mentioned in this book. One of the main reasons that victims do not disclose the abuse is the perceived or actual lack of support from family members. Some victims fear that they will not be believed, or that they will be believed but also blamed.

There are many parents who, for various reasons, cannot be available to meet their children's needs on an emotional level. Reasons for this include immaturity, lack of parenting skills, personality disorders, addictions, disinterest, mental illness, denial, and a perception of "parenting" as consisting of simply the provision of food, shelter, clothing, and toys. It is often the children or adolescents from these types of families who are vulnerable to becoming sexually abused, because the perpetrator will play on the victim's unfulfilled emotional needs while he is in the process of soliciting and grooming his victim.

Many parents, when learning that their child or teenager has been sexually abused, will initially respond as though supportive of the victim, but will eventually turn it all around and blame the victim for being somehow, some way, responsible for what happened. This results in a terrible feeling of abandonment for the victim because:

1.   The parent(s) who should have been there to prevent the abuse from happening in the first place were not there;

2.   The parent(s) who need to support the victim and help him or her with re-empowerment are not doing that.

Child and teenaged victims who cannot rely on their own parents for emotional support in effect have nobody. Perpetrators are proven correct with regard to having previously warned the victim that "Bad things will happen if you tell anybody," or, "Nobody will ever believe you." Additionally, the victim's own self-blame is reinforced and (s)he believes that (s)he is a "bad person" who is responsible for the whole situation. Many victims prefer to allow the abuse to continue, knowing that the abuse may be less painful to tolerate than non-support by their own parents.

Parentified Children

A parentified child is, in effect, a "parent" to his or her own parent(s), having been placed in this role by one or both of them. (S)he has been forced to assume a pre-mature adult position and to forego a normal childhood or adolescence in favor of taking care of the adults' needs. The extreme manifestation of this occurs in incestuous relationships between a parent and child whereby the parent uses the child to meet his or her own sexual needs. Responsibilities for the parentified child exceed that of age-appropriate expectations, since the parent becomes dependent upon the child to take care of him or her on an adult level. For example, there is the little boy who becomes the proverbial "man of the house" or the girl who becomes her mother's "housekeeper" after a divorce. Parentified children sometimes find it difficult to have normal relationships with their peers, and instead are attracted to older individuals. The parentified child has been taught to place others' needs ahead of their own. This sets the child up to be taken advantage of by self-serving adults such as sexual predators who are on the lookout for exactly this type of victim.

Failure to Protect Children from Perpetrators

Some parents have been known to "look the other way" despite gut-feelings that something just isn't right with their child. This happens often in incest cases, where one spouse is sexually abusing a child and the other spouse is in total denial of it. Reasons for this include:

People Who Can't Be Without A Partner: In cases where a parent's partner is abusing a child, the parent's priorities might be centered around the partner as opposed to the child(ren). These people are lacking in self-esteem to the point that they believe they cannot live without a partner—even a bad one is better than none at all. Sometimes, as in domestic violence cases, a parent has been dominated into submission by the partner's violent behavior.

Parents Who Are In Denial: Parents who have known the perpetrator for a long time may prefer to remain in denial—for example, "Father Bob is so nice to the kids…" Being a trusted friend of the family gives the perpetrator another advantage in that this provides easy access to his victim. One sex offender priest would often obtain his victim's parents' permission to take their daughter to rock concerts, movies, and other outings. In actuality, most of the time he would take the girl to a motel room or other pre-arranged location for the purpose of using drugs and having sex.

Parents Who "Hope" Nothing Is Going On: Some parents have a suspicion that something out of the ordinary might be happening between their child and an adult professional, but do not bother to take any action to investigate their suspicions. They may be afraid of "looking stupid" or of being accused of making "false accusations," so they assume that it is easier to just "hope" that nothing is going on.

Violence In The Home

Physical abuse in the home environment, whether of the adult partner or children, should be a warning sign. Some states now require a suspected child abuse report form to be filed with Child Protective agencies if it is suspected that a child has *witnessed* physical violence occurring in the home.

Addictions

Families in which one or both parents have alcohol and/or drug addictions are an indication that some level of emotional neglect or abuse of the children also exists. Adults whose priority is getting high, partying, and maintaining their substance abuse habits do not have the presence of mind to meet their children's emotional and psychological needs.

Parents with Personality Disorders

Parents who have personality disorders such as those previously described in this book place their children at-risk for becoming victims of sexual abuse. Most individuals with personality disorders are self-centered and incapable of having a healthy relationship with anyone—including their own children.

Parents Who Refuse Therapy

Certain parents tend to identify the child or teenager as the "problem" and will refuse to participate in therapy or might initially attend therapy but eventually drop out. Some of these parents have actually told therapists, "Little Johnny is the problem. Fix him!" while detaching from the whole process. If parents do not make an effort to collaborate in their child's treatment or follow-up as to their child's progress (or lack of it) in therapy, it is very likely that they are not collaborating in or following-up on other aspects of their child's life.

Dysfunctional Parenting Styles

During my interviews with victims of abuse by professionals, a recurring pattern emerged with regard to their family dynamics: the victims all felt that certain parenting techniques played a major part in setting them up for eventual abuse

- **Authoritarian Attitude:** Parents should not expect unquestioning compliance from their kids. The kids are not in the military. They should be allowed to "question authority" as this is part of the learning and developing process.

  Victim Account #1: My parents would always say to me in response to my asking why I should do things a certain way, "Never mind why— just do what I tell you!"

  Victim Account #2: My father used to tell me, 'Don't argue with me or I'll kick your ass!"

  Victim Account #3: "Our parents made us say 'Yes, sir,' and 'Yes, ma'am,' to them. We got in trouble if we didn't."

- **Lack of Respect for Kids' Feelings:** The same parents

who demand unquestioning compliance from their kids also insist that the kids show unconditional respect for them. However, they will attempt to suppress any of the kids' emotions with which they themselves are uncomfortable. Some parents will not allow kids to cry or express anger.

Victim Account #1: My parents hated it when we (kids) cried. They would say, "Stop crying or I will give you something to really cry about!"

Victim Account #2: One time, while I was playing a board game with my mom when I was about nine years old, she told me not to smile. I was smiling because I had more points than she did and was on the verge of possibly winning the game. What good is winning if you're not allowed to feel excited about it?

Victim Account #3: "My father used to call me names—e.g., Stupid' and 'Lazy,' but would hit me if I ever expressed anger by yelling at him not to call me names."

- **Use of Inappropriate Discipline:** Too often, violent types of punishment are used as consequences for non-violent misbehaviors. Parents will think nothing of using a belt or paddle to discipline their children—however, if that same parent were to use that belt or paddle on another adult, (s)he may be looking at a possible jail sentence because the object in question would be considered a weapon. Some states have enacted child abuse laws which make it illegal for parents to use certain types of discipline on a consistent basis. Using an object to physically discipline a child teaches the child

to tolerate abuse. It can also set children up to use violence to solve problems. In my research for my doctoral
dissertation, *Parental Discipline Styles and Violence of
Juvenile Crime* (Austin, 1995), I examined specific discipline styles and types of crimes committed by juve-
niles incarcerated in a juvenile detention facility. The
findings indicated that a significant percentage of the
children who had been subjected to harsh and violent
forms of punishment by parents were incarcerated for
committing violent crimes such as murder, armed robbery, drive by shootings, assault with deadly weapons,
and battery, than for non-violent types of crimes. By
comparison, the children who did not experience harsh
or violent discipline were incarcerated for non-violent
crimes such as curfew violations, probation violations,
drunk in public, and malicious mischief. Very few of
these children had committed violent crimes.

- **Not Allowing A Kid to Develop An Identity:** Victims
describe how one or both parents would not allow them
to develop an identity. Some parents attempted to shape
their kids into carbon copies of themselves via unrealistic expectations. Others attempted to compete with
their kids, thus making them feel worthless.

Victim Account #1: "My father refused to pay my
college tuition, because he claimed to have financial
difficulties, so I paid my tuition by taking out student
loans. When I got my Bachelor's and Master's degrees
after years of hard work, my father somehow managed
to come up with the money to purchase Bachelor's
and Master's degrees for himself from one of those
mail-order degree-mills. I realized that the real reason

he didn't want to pay my tuition was because he was afraid I'd become smarter than him, and he was trying to compete with me."

Victim Account #2: "My mom pushed me to become a lawyer. I rebelled against this because I wanted to be a musician. I felt guilty for not living up to my mom's expectations and eventually dropped out of school altogether."

- **Favoritism:** Favoring one child over the others and/or designation of one as the "black sheep" of the family. No child should ever be given the message, "I love you less than your sisters and brothers." The child who feels less-loved may be likely to look for love elsewhere and end up finding an illusion of it in a relationship with a sexual predator.

  Victim Account #1: "At my house, my sister could do no wrong. It was like she was dad's favorite."

  Victim Account #2: "My mom used to always say to me, 'Why can't you be more like your brother?' "

- **Mixed-Messages:** Parents should be congruent in their communications with their kids. The parent who tells one child that he loves him or her while at the same time showing favoritism to another child is sending a mixed-message. Likewise the parent who says something to a child and makes a different statement to a third party in the presence of the child.

  Victim Account: "One of my mom's friends handed my sister and I each a Christmas present when we were little kids. Mother immediately would say to us,

"What do you say? Can't you say 'thank you'?" without giving us a chance to respond independently. When we thanked the person, mom would tell her friend, "You shouldn't have done that! These kids don't know what it's like not to have anything!" Both of us had conflicting feelings for years; part of us thought that we didn't deserve to be given gifts, and another part of us tried to justify receiving them just based on the fact that it was Christmas."

- **Perfectionism:** Parents need to allow kids to make age-appropriate mistakes and learn from them. We all make mistakes. In a perfect world there would not be erasers on pencils.

  Victim Account #1: "My parents expected me to make straight-A's in school when I was a kid. I'd get put on restriction for anything less than a perfect report card."

  Victim Account #2: : "Once I brought home a straight-A report card when I was in the first grade. I didn't know that an "A" was the highest grade you could get. My parents told me that I 'could do better'."

- **Inappropriate Interpersonal Boundaries:** Parents with boundary issues of their own sometimes tend to establish inappropriate ones within the family structure. This can consist of enmeshment—where everybody knows everybody else's business and there is virtually no privacy—or disengagement, whereby everybody goes off and does their own thing without any accountability to anyone else.

  Victim Account #1: "In my family nobody had any privacy. My parents wrote down on the wall calendar every time that they had sex."

Victim Account #2: "Us kids weren't allowed to close our bedroom doors. If we ever did, our parents would freak out."

Victim Account #3: "My mom didn't have a clue as to what was going on, when we were teenagers. She was too much into her own thing. A lot of times I'd go spend a few days at a friend's house and she never knew I was gone."

- **Covert Incest:** : This is the non-physical dynamic of incestuous behavior. It can consist of parents being naked in front of their kids, making inappropriate sexual comments or jokes to the kids, flirting and/or being seductive with the kids, being jealous of a teenaged son or daughter's boyfriend or girlfriend, and placing a kid in a "spouse" or "partner" role.

Victim Account: "My mother used to be so jealous of my girlfriends when I was in high school. Whenever I'd take one of them out to dinner or to the show, she'd make comments like, 'You take her out to dinner—but you never take ME out! What is wrong with you?'"

- **Parents Who Are "Too Busy"**: Parents who are consistently too busy to spend quality time with their kids, for whatever reason, may be glad to be "relieved" of this obligation by another adult—teacher, coach, priest, etc.—who might be too eager to do so.

Victim Account #1: "My parents seemed always to have time for work-related social priorities, but rarely made time to attend school plays, baseball games, and stuff like that."

Victim Account #2: "When my parents managed to find time to attend school functions, they whined and complained as though it was the biggest imposition on them. Yet, they would expect my sisters and I to get all dressed up to be shown off at their company parties."

Victim Account #3: "My mom didn't bother going to stuff that my brother and I were into—she was either going to drug parties, or crashed on the couch coming down off of crack."

- **Expecting Kids to Keep Secrets:** A parent who confides secrets in a child and expects the child to keep those secrets from the other parent is asking for trouble all the way around. This sets the child up to be the bad guy in a catch-22 situation: (s)he is bad if (s)he discloses the secrets, and bad if (s)he keeps them and the other parent finds out that (s)he did. A child or teenager has no business being their parents' confidante.

Victim Account#1: "My mom expected me to keep her marriage to my step-dad a secret from my father because if my father discovered it he would no longer have to pay child support, as per the conditions of their divorce settlement."

Victim Account #2: "My dad used to deal cocaine. My sister and I were expected not to tell our mom about it."

- **Deceptive Manipulation Tactics:** Specifically, I am referring to the use of shame, guilt, fear, and lies in attempts to control kids. This is not parenting—it is coercion. It teaches kids that parents cannot be trusted or relied upon.

Victim Account #1: "I was born with a dark brown birthmark at the base of my right thumb which looked like a large mole. When I was little, I asked my mother why there was a "brown spot" on my hand. Her response was to look at me really condescendingly and tell me, 'That means you have a bad hand. It means that you steal things.' I had never stolen anything! I went through childhood believing that I was born bad, and not understanding why. It wasn't until I was a teenager I realized my mother was full of shit, and only because my friends explained to me what a birthmark really was."

Victim Account #2: "My parents had a habit of consistently undermining my accomplishments. It didn't matter what I did or how well I did it, they always had to criticize me. I was actually surprised when I passed the fingerprint clearance to become an FBI agent. All of my teenage years I believed that I was such a "bad" person that it was confusing to me that the fingerprint clearance did not reveal a "secret" criminal record of some sort."

• **Non-Involvement & Sabotage**: "My parents were divorced and basically weren't there for me. I lived with my dad, who was a real Narcissist. He either competed with me or sabotaged my progress toward my goals and ambitions. My mom was detached from everything and didn't participate in the process of my attempts to accomplish things. As a result, I didn't feel that I deserved anything. I didn't graduate from high school. When I got my first job, I developed severe anxiety and obsessed, daily, that I would be fired. When I got my first apartment, I worried that I would be evicted. When I finally got my Associate degree after going to college for five years, I became very depressed and suicidal. I couldn't tell my parents that my graduation was pending. I didn't tell them until after my finals were over. That way, they couldn't take it away from me."

BEHAVIORAL INDICATORS

Symptoms Which Do Not Improve Over Time

A huge red-flag should be problem behavior and/or symptoms manifested by the victim which do not improve despite months or even years of therapy by the same therapist. Consider the problem-teenager from a dysfunctional family who is truant from school, uses drugs, gets involved in fights, and has been seeing the same therapist in individual therapy sessions for a number of years— with no improvement. In fact, assume that perhaps the behavior has become worse than it initially was, to the point that the teenager has served time in the Juvenile Detention Facility on several occasions. School personnel, police, and probation officers should ask themselves and each other "With all of the counseling this student receives, why isn't (s)he making any improvement?" Any or all of these mandated reporters should take the time to interview the student about his or her life situation and attempt to determine why therapy has not been effective. Perhaps it may be time to employ the services of a different therapist. If there is in fact sexual abuse occurring, the student might eventually be willing to disclose this to a therapist who is skilled in facilitating such disclosure.

Another red flag should be the therapist who makes no attempt to collaborate with other agencies or professionals in the child's treatment, and who does not keep the child's parents or teachers apprised of the child's progress in therapy. A therapist who does not have treatment plans documented, or case progress notes charted, should also raise major suspicions.

A Professional who "Favors" A Particular Child

Serious attention should be given to the professional who spends an unusual amount of time alone with one particular child or teenager. For example, the school counselor who keeps one particular student after school several times per week "for assistance with homework" or "for counseling" without the parents' collaboration, and sometimes without the parents' knowledge. Or the young priest who "dates" a teenaged girl whose parents don't allow her to attend school dances or date boys her own age. Teenagers often perceive these professionals as "cool" or "hip," especially if the professional allows them to get away with conduct which they would not normally get away with elsewhere.

Parents and other professionals should be alert to these situations and *not allow a child to be alone with anyone who acts suspiciously!*

Depression

As stated previously, keeping a sexual abuse "secret" inflicts a whole different set of responsibilities on a child or teenager in that many people's lives can depend on whether or not the secret is kept. The victim cannot verbalize his or her frustrations about the "relationship" to friends or family. (S)he cannot even indicate to anyone that the "relationship" exists. Any emotional, physical, or verbal abuse from the perpetrator must be dealt with by the victim in silence. Likewise any fears resulting from threats made by the perpetrator.

Unverbalized feelings have two possible outlets: behavioral acting-out, or internalization whereby they become directed at the inner self and can manifest as symptoms of chronic depression. One victim described the chronic depression as painful and frustrating: "Like trying to yell in a dream but not having a voice. You feel like you don't want to live, but you don't want to die, either. You just want the pain to go away." Victims have been known to engage in self-mutilation behaviors as a type of "compromise" between living and dying, and to attempt to transform the inner pain to something more tangible and "real." Others have been known to develop eating disorders to as to have a sense of "control" over their own body.

Sexual Acting-Out

Children who seem sexually precocious and display inappropriate sexual behaviors may have been sexually abused. Likewise with teenagers who dress over-suggestively, become promiscuous or engage in prostitution.

Withdrawn or Passive Behavior

Children or adolescents who are unusually quiet and withdrawn might have something on their mind and should not be ignored. It is too easy for teachers, school staff, and even school resource officers to focus on the disruptive, aggressive kids and disregard the extremely quiet ones. Don't assume that the "quiet ones" don't have anything to say.

"RED FLAGS" FOR POLICE

Cases Involving A Minor or Young Adult and an Adult Professional: Whether brought to the attention of law enforcement by third-parties, the victim, or even the adult professional, the all-important question should be "WHY is there a problem between this juvenile or young adult and this professional?" Police should take complaints against professionals by minors and young adults seriously. Even if the situation appears to be that of a civil matter in which police have no jurisdiction, police should be supportive and suggest to the victim that (s)he consult with an attorney who specializes in the matter at issue.

Complaints by the Professional: Cases in which an adult professional has sought the assistance of law enforcement might actually be situations in which the perpetrator has set the victim up to be the "bad guy."

Police should be aware of the possibility of an attempt by a perpetrator to deflect investigation into his own conduct by pointing the finger at the victim, and avoid rushing to judgment with regard to identifying the victim as nothing but a troublemaker

Behavioral "Patterns" by the Victim: Here, I am referring to teenagers or young adults who come to the attention of the police because of some type of problem which consists of repeat offenses, or appears to be suggestive of a possible "modus operandi". For example, a teenager who on multiple occasions is suspected of having vandalized his or her psychotherapist's office building may have actually committed these acts of malicious mischief as an indirect cry for help. Police should not ignore the possibility that the victim might be too afraid to make a direct statement about having been sexually abused and hopes that the police will discover the perpetrator's crime on their own. If the police discover the crime as the result of their own investigation, this relieves the victim of the burden of, and guilt associated with, having to "snitch" on the perpetrator—especially if the perpetrator is a relative or friend of the family.

Evidence of Stockholm Syndrome: Police should familiarize themselves with the features of Stockholm Syndrome and the situations in which it is likely to develop. Stockholm Syndrome is the number one survival strategy for victims of abuse and interpersonal violence.

Features:

- The victim may perceive the abuser as some kind of "hero." In situations where the abuser is a trusted professional, the abuser may have played the role of catalyst in terms of providing the victim with a means of relief or escape from a negative situation, such as a dysfunctional home environment. The abuser may have provided the victim with a means of avoiding an impending negative situation, such as the threat of going to a juvenile detention center.

- An emotional bonding has occurred between the victim and the abuser.

- The victim loses appropriate perspective and accepts the abuser's reasons or justifications for the abuse.

- The victim seeks approval from and is sympathetic toward the abuser.

- The victim supports, assists, and defends the abuser's. The abusive conduct is minimized and/or not acknowledged by the victim for what it actually is.

- The victim is unable to take advantage of opportunities to escape. The victim cannot just "walk away from" the situation because (s)he believes there is no escape.

Precipitating Situations:

- **A power-imbalance exists** whereby the abuser is the person with the greater power. The abuser uses his power to hold the victim emotionally hostage. This can occur in situations such as: pimp-prostitute, parent-child, teacher-student, therapist-patient, employer-employee, hostage-captor.

- **The victim believes that a threat exists** with regard to his/her own safety and/or the safety of others. Further, the victim believes that (s)he is responsible for the safety of him or her self and/or others.

- **The abuser is alternately kind and abusive.** This has the effect of intermittent behavioral reinforcement, in that the victim doesn't know when the "kindness" might be forthcoming.

Notes:

NOTES:

CHAPTER TEN:

CHANGING THE LAWS

The terrible and prolific crime of sexual abuse needs to be addressed more effectively at the State and Federal levels. Certain laws tend to favor sexual predators' rights over those of the victims' and, therefore, should be changed.

STATUTE OF LIMITATIONS: "SOL"

The Statute of Limitations (also referred to as the "SOL") is the time period within which criminal prosecution or civil litigation must be commenced after the commission of a crime or the infliction of personal injury. For lack of a better term, the SOL is a type of "deadline" after which civil or criminal action may not be pursued. Reasons for establishing SOL's include the possibility that witnesses might re-locate or die; people's memories of an event become unreliable over time; and fairness to the defendant. Each crime and civil matter has its own SOL, and these vary between States.

As an example, the SOL for certain civil causes of action might be as follows:

- Personal Injury based on negligence = two years;

- Breach of an oral contract = two years;

- Slander or libel = one year;

- Medical malpractice = three years from the date of injury; or one year from the date the plaintiff discovers the injury;

- Childhood sexual abuse = three years after the victim realizes that (s)he has been damaged physically or psychologically; or eight years after the victim's eighteenth

birthday. Both would apply regardless of the victim's
age at the time (s)he files a lawsuit.

Criminal statutes of limitations might range from one to three
years for misdemeanors, and six to eight years for felonies.

The acronym "SOL" is also slang for "Shit-Out-of-Luck." In
many sexual abuse cases involving delayed reporting, victims find
themselves in exactly that position—Shit-Out-of-Luck. It can
take years—often decades—for victims to realize that the "relationship" in which they were involved with a trusted professional
was sexual abuse. It can take years for victims to develop the courage to report the abuse, for various reasons. In these cases, the
SOL is to the advantage of the perpetrator in that justice is, in
effect, on his side. As far as the victim is concerned, this is a situation where time does NOT heal, but instead makes things worse.
The victim is the one who ultimately ends up serving a life sentence from the impact and effects of the abuse. The perpetrator,
in the meantime, has managed to escape prosecution, and is free
to continue his behavior with other victims. It is for these reasons
that the Statute of Limitations needs to be abolished for childhood sexual abuse cases.

If we consider that the mindset of a child molester is identical
to that of a serial killer, with basically identical modus operandi
in terms of planning the commission of the crime and hiding evidence, the serial killer and child molester can be considered psychologically one and the same. Their crime is murder. One kills
the physical body. The other kills the person's spiritual self and
capacity to live a normal life. No amount of restitution can compensate for the damage in either situation. Like the serial killer,
the child molester typically has multiple victims. Neither will
stop until he is arrested. There is no Statute of Limitations for
the crime of murder in any state. Murderers are well aware that
the passage of time will not relieve them from having to face the

eventual legal consequences of their crimes. In contrast, Statutes of Limitations exist for the crime of sexual abuse with children in all states. Child molesters are well aware that time will eventually relieve them from having to face the criminal, and sometimes civil, consequences of their crimes. There is something definitely wrong with that picture

GAG ORDERS

"Gag orders" are agreements or mandatory conditions of a settlement of a lawsuit whereby the plaintiff is prohibited from discussing the causes of action against the defendant, the amount of damages or settlement awarded by the court, and the disposition of the case. The purpose of gag orders is to protect the defendant's privacy by further silencing the victims. Victims are, in effect, paid to keep quiet. This is ironic, considering that much of the damage suffered by the victims results from having to keep quiet about the abuse, in the first place!

Gag orders need to be abolished. The First Amendment of the United States Constitution clearly states, "No law can abridge the freedom of speech." Citizens have the right to be informed about sexual predators because of the strong likelihood of repeat-offending. Victims of sexual abuse should have the right to speak out about their experiences and not be paid to further keep the secret so as to avoid invasion of the offender's privacy. These "confidentiality" conditions of settlement are unconstitutional, against public policy, and should not be enforced by the courts. The safety of potential victims should clearly outweigh the desire for privacy on the defendant's part, especially when the offender is a trusted professional who has unrestricted access to vulnerable children and young adults on a daily basis, and is unlikely to stop his behavior.

Victims should have the right to identify their abusers publicly, if they so desire, including abusers who have settled with the victims in civil litigation or out-of-court compromises

GOVERNMENTAL IMMUNITY

Under the doctrine of Governmental Immunity, certain government agencies such as public schools and hospitals are held less accountable for their actions in civil lawsuits simply because these agencies are funded by citizens' tax dollars. A justification for this is that abolishing governmental immunity would result in an overwhelming amount of lawsuits against public agencies. A disadvantage for victims of sexual abuse by public school personnel, or government agency staff, is that many attorneys are reluctant to take these cases because there is very little or no money in them. A victim who has been sexually abused by a priest or nun in a Catholic school stands a significantly better chance of recovering financially in a civil lawsuit than if (s)he had been sexually abused by a public school employee. Apparently, religious and certain other non-profit organizations are held to a higher standard due to their tax-exempt status.

Governmental Immunity should be abolished so that sex offenders in both public and private agencies are held equally accountable.

NOTES:

NOTES:

CHAPTER ELEVEN:

CONCLUSION

The result of sexual abuse is long-term psychological and emotional damage. This can affect childrens' and adolescents' capacity for normal development, and predispose them to re-victimization. Parents can inadvertently set children up to become victims of sexual abuse via dysfunctional parenting styles which do not foster children's self-esteem.

Victims of sexual abuse have a few options available for taking action against the perpetrator. These options include reporting the professional to his or her licensing or credentialing agency; reporting the incident(s) to the local District Attorney for criminal prosecution; applying for financial compensation from the State Victims of Crime Assistance Fund; and filing a civil lawsuit for personal injury damages.

Victims who file civil or criminal complaints against their abusers can expect the legal process to be painful and drawn-out. Defense attorneys will use numerous cut-throat tactics before and during trial in attempts to destroy the victim's credibility. Defense counsel will try to pressure the victim into dropping the case altogether, before it ever gets to trial. The Statute of Limitations protects offenders in cases of delayed reporting. As a result, victims typically feel as though they are being further violated by the System.

The author concludes that, in order to more effectively deal with the problem of sexual abuse, laws need to be changed so as to empower the victims, versus provide sex offenders with loopholes and hiding places. Mandated reporters of suspected abuse need to be more strictly held to their legal responsibility.

Finally, more thorough screening procedures need to be enacted by educational and training programs, seminars, and licensing boards, so as to identify individuals with severe character flaws before they have a chance to become professionals in the mental health, clergy, and law enforcement fields who abuse their power.

Notes:

NOTES:

RESOURCES

SNAP

SNAP (Survivors' Network of those Abused by Priests) was founded by Chicago's Barbara Blaine in 1989. Since then, SNAP has helped thousands of survivors. SNAP is the largest, oldest, and most active support group for women and men wounded by religious authority figures (priests, ministers, bishops, deacons, nuns and others). SNAP is an independent and confidential organization, with no connections with the church or church officials. Snap provides a safe and productive outlet for the passion many survivors feel toward preventing future abuse.

If you have been victimized by clergy, please know that you are not alone. You can get better. You can reach out to others who have been hurt just like you have. Together, we can heal one another.

Our website exists to provide support and knowledge to all victims of clergy abuse, to help educate the public, and to help ensure that in future generations children will be safe

www.snapnetwork.org

[From www.snapnetwork.org *Welcome!*
Used with permission of SNAP.]

THE POLICE COMPLAINT CENTER

Complaint Service:

Our staff will assist you in reporting police misconduct to the appropriate authorities. This service is free.

Traditional Investigative Services and Searches:

Do you need a private investigator to help with your case? We have 10 licensed private investigators available 24/7. We specialize in police misconduct cases. We also provide traditional search and investigative services.

Walking Tall Service:

How did you feel after your police encounter? Have yu ever wanted to ask the officer why he did it? What were his motives? Can he explain himself? Why did he misstate your conduct in his report?

In a democracy, citizens are entitled to have questions answered by public officials when evidence of misconduct is present. This is especially true in police misconduct cases. Unfortunately, many victims never get answers. There has to be a solution to this problem. We think we have it.

We will contact the police officer that you are accusing of misconduct by telephone or in person. We will audio and/or video record the officer's responses to the questions you raise concerning his treatment of you or a family member. Even if the officer refused to explain his behavior during the incident, we are not afraid to get answers now.

Investigative Reconstruction Service:

Don't rely on the police version of events.

Have you ever watched the hit shows *HBO Autopsy*, and *A & E Investigative Reports* or the CBS series *CSI* and wished that you could bring the sort of expertise used in these shows to your own case?

When HBO's Dr. Michael Baden explains how the crime was committed you are certain that you have a good idea who the guilty and innocent are. Why? Because Dr. Baden is an expert. When he talks people take him seriously. Similarly, the detectives acting as the experts on *Investigative Reports* are convincing when they tell you the shot was fired from close range. We look forward to someone with experience explaining what really happened at the crime scene.

How would your case benefit from a retired police detective going over the details and questioning the officer that wrote the false report? If you would like to have a police detective explore your case and point out the contradictions between what really happened and what ended up in a police report, we can help. Our licensed private investigators are retired police detectives from New Jersey, New York, and Los Angeles area police departments.

Our detectives will come to your community to investigate any act of misconduct committed by a police officer.

Investigative reconstruction allows our staff to analyze and highlight contradictions and false statements made by police officers in their reports and courtroom testimony.

We will interview you and any other involved victims to record your version of events. Your case will be given the same expertise and investigative analysis used by law enforcement officials.

Our detectives will demonstrate that officers did not have a legal basis for their conduct. We will conduct an investigative re-enactment going over every portion of your case. Your evidence will be used to generate a short film explaining the details of your case.

Your evidence and video will be used to create a DVD which will be delivered to the Justice Department in Washington, D.C. Your video will also be distributed to important community members, city officials, and others at your discretion. Your video may also be aired on public access television or used to request a broader investigation by a network news organization such as Dateline, 2020, or 60 Minutes.

Other Services:

- We can locate other victims of the officer that mistreated you. They may testify in your case.

- We can file a complaint against prison officials and correctional offices.

- We can send an investigator to you to investigate your complaint of misconduct.

- We can provide security if you are being persistently harassed by the police.

- We can obtain the personnel file of the officer or deputy.

- We can test your police department for abuse and misconduct.

- We can locate and identify police officers that refuse to provide their name or badge number.

- We can request that the police agency lose accreditation for failure to investigate citizen complaints.

- We can assist you with the steps you must take to sue the police without an attorney.

- We can get you legal support within 24 hours if you need an attorney. We will research your legal matter and find the best attorneys in the area to help you.

The Police Complaint Center
www.policeabuse.org
Tel.: (202) 250-3499
Fax: (202) 318- 8158

[From www.policeabuse.org *Services*. Used with permission of the Police Complaint Center.]

Online Resources

Child Sexual Abuse

Megan's Law Website / Registered CA Sex Offenders
www.meganslaw.ca.gov

Child Protection Specialists
www.yellodyno.com

National Association to Protect Children
www.protect.org

Sexual Predators
www.perverted-justice.com

Oprah Winfrey Show
www.oprah.com

Civil Rights Group / Child Pornography
www.ricoforkids.org

Stop Educator Sexual Abuse, Misconduct, and Exploitation
www.sesamenet.org

America's Most Wanted
www.americasmostwanted.com

National Crime Victims Bar Association
www.victimbar.org

Family Violence Prevention Fund
www.endabuse.org

Rape Victim Advocacy
www.rapevictimadvocates.org

Abuse By Clergy

Catholics for Justice
www.Catholics4Justice.com

Bishop Accountability
www.bishop-accountability.org

Celibacy Is the Issue / Fr. John Shuster
www.rentapriest.com

Gay & Lesbian Alliance Against Defamation
www.glaad.org

Police Corruption

Policing the Police
www.copwatch.com

Bad Cop News
www.badcopnews.com

Professional Abuse

Professional Sexual Misconduct
www.AdvocateWeb.org

Therapy Exploitation
www.therapyabuse.org

Athlete Protection
www.silent-edge.org

Recommended Reading

Clark, Howard. (1993). *Love's Blood*. St. Martin's Press, New York

Doyle, Thomas, A.W.R. Sipe, & Patrick J. Wall. (2006). *Sex, Priests, and Secret Codes: The Catholic Church's 2000-Year Paper Trail of Sexual Abuse*. Volt Press, Los Angeles, CA

Juarez, Juan Antonio. (2004). *Brotherhood of Corruption*. Chicago Review Press, Chicago, IL

Lyken, David. (1998). *A Tremor In the Blood: Uses and Abuses of the Lie Detector*. Perseus Books, New York, NY

Payson, Eleanor. (2002). *The Wizard of Oz and Other Narcissists*. Juilan Day Publications, Royal Oak, MI

Quinn, Michael. (2005). *The Police Code of Silence: Walking With the Devil*. Quinn & Associates. www.booksbyquinn.com

Samenow, Stanton E. (2004). *Inside the Criminal Mind*. Crown Publishers, New York, NY

NOTES:

NOTES:

Printed in the United States
By Bookmasters